HOW TO PAY "WHOLESALE" FOR COLLEGE

5th Edition

Financial aid and scholarship "loopholes" that ANY family can use to qualify for 52.4% off the cost of college, even if you think, "It's no use - families like us never get financial aid!"

Andy Lockwood

Forward to the 5th Edition

Lots of stuff has come down the pike in the college world, especially the scandal involving Felicity Huffman, Lori Loughlin and a few dozen other wealthy parents, not to mention the parents in the Chicagoland area who (legally) changed the guardianship of their children in order to qualify for more aid.

Most of the news coverage was about the college admissions hijinks, and well covered by the media (and by my other most recent, opportunistic book, *How to Get Into Your Dream College Without Lying, Bribing or Photoshopping.)*[1]

However, there have been other changes pertaining to financial aid. The process is more complicated than ever, despite initiatives such as the mobile FAFSA (spoiler alert: not recommended) and the FSA ID - a secure method for parents and students to sign their FAFSAs electronically.

The IRS overhauled the 2018 1040 (tax return), but that won't change much, if anything, significant about the financial aid process *per se.*

College costs have continued to rise since the last edition of this book, but tuition discounting is also on the upswing. The average

---

[1] (On Amazon and makes a thoughtful holiday gift. Run, don't walk.)

at private colleges is currently (2019) 52.4%, according to the National Association of Collegiate Business Officers.

Does that mean that EVERYONE will get 50% plus off?

Of course not, I'm disappointed that you even thought to ask me that. Embarrassing.

OK, seriously, what that DOES mean - and this is the main point of this book that I hope you absorb - that paying "Full Boat" is a choice. NOT an obligation.

Herein, you'll see how any family - even six and seven-figure earners - can slash their college costs. We'll look at how to identify more generous colleges, the need-based financial aid formula, tips for qualifying for merit aid, how to negotiate with colleges, and even some tax stuff thrown in for good measure.

In other words, there's a little somethin'-somethin' for everybody in this here "Instant Classic!"

And, if you want to go "deeper" - to get more information on how YOU can create a winning game plan to master the college admissions and/or college financial aid and scholarships beast, please visit our website, www.LockwoodCollegePrep.com, where you can schedule a complimentary College Strategy Session (phone call), which we normally charge $499 for. But it's free because you read this book..

You'll also see a treasure trove of free and not free resources on our website, including a schedule of upcoming webinars and live local to the NY area workshops.

Thanks for reading this book, and, if you decide to advance your Financial Aid Jedi training and reach out to us for more help, my team and I look forward to speaking with you.

Sincerely,

Andy Lockwood
Long Island's Greatest Unindicted College Advisor

NOW FOR A RIVETING DISCLAIMER

We're each adults, right? So it should go without saying that this book is NOT PERSONALIZED ADVICE. I'm using all caps not because I'm shouting, but to emphasize that the general strategies described inside are not a substitute for actual, advisor-to-client, one-on-one advice.

So please consider this book as a general guide and consult a qualified advisor if you have any questions about your specific situation instead of blindly trusting every morsel out of my mouth, the way the wife and kids do. [2]

This book is not legal, financial or any other advice. And you should not rely on the examples of successful clients described herein. Just because they achieved great results, doesn't mean that you will. Your results could be equal, worse, or better.

I, my advisors and anyone else who contributed to this book, are in no way liable or responsible to you or any person for any damage or liability caused directly or indirectly by the information in this book.

So there.

---

[2] Not.

WHO THIS BOOK IS FOR

If you're uptight about the cost of college and your ability to afford to send your son or daughter to their Dream Colleges, this book should help you discover that you don't have to pay "Sticker Price."

If you have the lettuce to pay Full Boat, but have a tough time understanding WHY you should overpay, when so many families figure out how to get discounts, this book if also for you.

This book isn't theory. It's based on close to 20 years advising families with college-bound teens, not only on how to GET IN to a top college, but also how to qualify for fat, juicy merit scholarships and need-based aid.

You're about to learn actual tips and tactics that we use on a near-daily basis that YOU might be able to implement to save a few thousand smackers. I'm not holding anything back, this book contains everything I think you need to know.

No unproven theories or fluff here, pal.

And who knows, maybe you'll get a chuckle or two along the way. (If you crack a smile there's a good chance that I was doubled over, guffawing at the same joke when I wrote it.[3])

---

[3] Typical. I am my own best audience.

I hope you find this book valuable and that, if you're interested, it serves as a conversation starter between you and me, if you're looking for help in paying for college, getting into college, or both!

Enjoy!

Andy Lockwood

Lockwood College Prep
135 Glenwood Road
Glenwood Landing, New York 11547-0535
516.882.5464
www.LockwoodCollegePrep.com

TABLE OF CONTENTS

INTRODUCTION

Let's talk turkey. I hate to be negative[4] but things are REALLY bleak for families with college-bound teens.

- College costs continue to skyrocket

- 40-50% (depending on the poll) of college graduates don't have a job that requires a college degree...TWO YEARS after graduation

- Student debt 1.5 Trillion at the time of writing - and defaults - are at nauseatingly high levels;

- PARENT debt and defaults are over the top and growing; and

- College is harder to get into than ever!

How's that for an opener?! Doesn't exactly inspire you to read more, does it?

Although these are real, not "alternative" facts or "Fake News," there's no reason you have to mortgage your house, or your retirement savings - up the eyeballs to afford to send your kiddo to a great school. Just bear with me and read on.

---

[4] That's a lie. I love insulting friends and family - it makes me feel better about myself.

What this book is all about

I'm going to lay out the actual, tested and proven tactics I use in my practice to help parents – particularly "Forgotten Middle Class" families — who think they can't qualify for any financial aid – cut their college costs by 25%, 33%, 50% or more.

Just so you know, you're getting these amazing, life-changing pearls of wisdom[5] at a fraction of the price that our premium private clients pay for one-on-one advice. Our consulting services currently range from $2,500-12,500, but you'll find all I "gots" in here, I have no interest in holding anything back or teasing you in any way.[6]

Here's who I had in mind when I cranked out the first edition of *How To Pay Wholesale For College,* and still have in mind:

- "Forgotten Middle Class" families who think *What drugs are YOU on? We can't qualify for anything, why bother applying!*

- Six and even seven-figure earning families who either don't have the lettuce to pay full boat, or have it but don't see the VALUE in paying it

---

[5] Modesty not included.

[6] But if you want the WHOLE story, send us your credit card! Not the info on your credit card, the actual card. Operators ("Butch") are standing by. KIDDING.

- Business Owners who can take advantage of a handful of unique "loopholes" in the rules

- Divorced or separated families who have special considerations in financial aid

- Guidance counselors, CPA's, educators, PTA moms, financial advisors, anyone who wants to help families under their charge but don't have the time or resources to obtain the requisite training

In a nutshell, this book is for anyone confused and stressed about how the hell THEY can possibly afford to send their kids to college!

If any of these sounds like you, let's dig in!

Warning for the Easily Offended

Wait, one more word of warning. There are hundreds of books on the topic of college funding. The best ones are informative, but 99% are on the dry side, like a textbook.

Moi, on the other hand, tried to make this book entertaining. Again, not easy, considering the subject matter.

I realize that some people don't think my jokes are funny. That's perfectly ok.[7] Please do not take my irreverent tone to mean that I'm making light of your situation. But if you are incapable of

---

[7] Yes, it's perfectly OK to be stupid. KIDDING. (Half-kidding.)

enjoying a little goof once in awhile, maybe you should stop reading this (nonrefundable) book now.

I wrote it this way to help you loosen up, chill out and free up your mind to the possibilities that you CAN obtain relief![8]

OK, enough chit-chat – let's go!

---

[8] And to amuse myself. Duh.

CHAPTER 1

How Does It All Work, Anyway?

Here is a SHORT explanation on how the whole financial aid process works. Because this is a summary, I am leaving a handful of less-important details out. So relax. I'll cover the important missing stuff in the rest of this book.

What is "Financial Aid?"

Many parents think the term "Financial Aid" refers to loans, only. It doesn't.

"Financial Aid" is a catch-all term that includes loans, work-study, and free stuff – grants and scholarships.

"Grants" usually refer to free money awarded based on "Financial Need," i.e. "how you look on paper based on income, assets, number of kids in college at the time, age and other factors.

The term "Scholarship" typically indicates merit-based awards, meaning money given for grades, scores, athletic ability, performing arts talent and so forth. (You'll see that many colleges use the term "Merit" loosely – they award money to non-academically elite, non-athletes and non-performing artists too.)

How Do You Apply for Financial Aid?

You apply by filling out forms and submitting them to the schools your child is applying to. Most people do this online, but I suppose some schools still accept hard copies.[9] The most common forms are:

The Free Application for Federal Student Aid, or FAFSA. The Federal form, required by all colleges. It's free.

Currently, the FAFSA is a little more than 100 questions, asking mostly about income, savings accounts and other tedious stuff designed to calculate how much you are able to afford for college, according to a bunch of nameless, faceless bureaucrats in the Department Of Education. You can trust them, right?

The directions are clear for the most part, but Pearl and I see mistakes all the time. I point out some of the biggies in a later chapter. Many stem from failing to read the directions accompanying each question, which is understandable, because they're written in Bureaucratic-ese, mostly.

This is the main reason why we recommend that you steer away from using the mobile FAFSA introduced in 2018-2019, by the

---

[9] Please submit them online, even if you have to drive your horse and buggy to a local library. You can opt for a paper copy, but the guys in the financial aid office will laugh at you behind your back.

way - it's hard enough to read the directions on the regular version.

The CSS Profile ("The Profile") is another popular, less common form, used by roughly 400 colleges in addition to - NOT in lieu of - the FAFSA. CSS Profile colleges are typically private schools with their own endowment money to dole out, instead of primarily Federal grants and loans offered by FAFSA only colleges

The Profile is a pain in the rumpus![10] It's more than 200 questions, and much more detailed than the FAFSA. And some colleges tack on additional, supplemental questions. Supplemental, NOSY questions, that is.

Why so cumbersome? Colleges with their own institutional endowment funds want more detail on your financial picture before they decide to commit their money to you. So they rake you over the coals, with all sorts of detailed questions NOT on the FAFSA, such as:

- The value of your retirement accounts (although they claim that retirement savings won't affect your eligibility)[11]

---

[10] Latin for *tuchus*

[11] I they don't penalize you for your retirement accounts, why do they ask about them? Answer: because they can! And because some schools ARE swayed by what you have socked away in your IRA or 401(k), I've witnessed it first-hand. (But most colleges ignore this info.)

- The fair market value of your home
- Your mortgage balances and monthly payments
- The year you bought your home and price paid
- How much you can afford to pay for college
- Whether you anticipate help from any other family members or other sources to help you pay for college
- Profit and Loss, Balance Sheet and other information about your business, if self-employed
- Whether you have savings in any of your OTHER kids' names
- More!

Here's the kicker: technically, you (Mom or Dad) should not complete this form, **your CHILD is supposed to fill out the Profile!**

Yes. YES. You read that correctly. Here's why:

The CSS Profile is made by the College Board – the same College Board that administers the SAT.

When your child registers for the PSAT, in Sophomore or Junior year, she creates a user name and password for the College Board. These login credentials are the same used to access the CSS Profile.

Brace yourself for some savvy advice from a high-priced college finance and admissions expert[12]:

Do NOT let your child fill out your financial aid forms!

(Unless you're comfortable turning over your tax returns, bank statements, etc. to young Johnny and trusting him to understand them.)

> RESOURCE: We cover the gory details about the entire financial aid process, soup-to-nuts, including key differences of the FAFSA and CSS Profile, in a free online workshop: www.FinancialAidWebcast.com

If you are a business owner whose child is applying to a school that takes the CSS Profile[13], you'll likely be required to complete and submit a Business/Farm Supplement[14], which consists of basic financial information that your accountant can handwrite.

Supplemental Forms

---

[12] I'm showing restraint. I could have said "devastatingly handsome" or "ruggedly built."

[13] Always check with each college on your list what forms it requires. Here's a link to a list of all CSS Profile schools published by the College Board: https://profileonline.collegeboard.org/prf/PXRemotePartInstitutionServlet/ PXRemotePartInstitutionServlet.srv

[14] Yes, "Farm." Try not to get any cow shit on your financial aid forms.

A small number of colleges require you to fill out their own, unique forms. They tend to be along the lines of a "CSS Profile Lite." Example: a FAFSA school may have a shorter supplemental form that asks about home equity and a few other items not covered by the FAFSA.

Check the website of each college on your list to see what forms are required...and WHEN.

When Do You Apply for Financial Aid?

The short answer is "Whenever a college tells you to." Because deadlines vary from school to school, there is no common due date for each college.

At the risk of beating a dead horse, I want to emphasize that THERE IS NO UNIVERSAL DEADLINE for each school, unlike tax deadlines such as April 15th. Each college has its own priority financial aid deadline. There is no shortcut, you must keep track of the deadlines yourself.

Here's something else that's dumb about the process: you apply BEFORE you know whether or not your child got into the colleges on his or her list. In other words, you apply to "purchase" your product – a degree – before you know how much it will cost.[15]

---

[15] Can you imagine buying a car or a home this way?

Most high school seniors submit their ADMISSIONS applications sometime in the fall, say October or November.[16]

Most FINANCIAL AID applications are submitted between October and February, in accordance with each college's financial aid Priority Deadlines.[17]

Note: most colleges have later deadlines for returning students, i.e. sophomores, juniors and seniors. Always check the financial aid section on your college's website.

Note Deux - this is also important - reminders about deadlines, forms, etc. for returning, upperclassmen students flows through the STUDENTS. So that means your son or daughter needs to check their email more frequently than "Each time the Cleveland Browns win the Super Bowl." [18] Otherwise, you could be in a world of hurt.

Yes - **you reapply for financial aid each year.** The first year is the most important, because it sets a precedent for the ensuing years. But you must reapply, because income can change from year to year, so can savings.

---

[16] The FAFSA used to become available January 1. Now it's October 1. Things change.

[17] Typically February 15th or March 1, but this is important to research on each school's website because Priority Deadlines vary. (I know I already covered this.)

[18] I'm a huge Pats fan. I can make fun of every other NFL team.

Back to the "Trust But Verify" concept - Pearl and I have seen and heard dozens of horror stories of parents missing deadlines - and losing out on financial aid they otherwise should have received - because their kids never forwarded them notices from their financial aid offices about due dates. Blech.

So **please monitor your kid's email box**, set up a separate one for both of you, or come up with your own strategy if you don't quite trust your son or daughter to stay on top of these communications.

CHAPTER 2

SHOULD YOU BOTHER APPLYING IF YOU HAVE DON'T HAVE A SNOWBALL'S SHOT IN HELL OF QUALIFYING?

Most of the time, yes. For two reasons:

1. You might be wrong about your snowball-in-hell chances, and
2. One or more of your colleges might require you to complete the FAFSA and CSS Profile to be eligible for MERIT scholarships.

There's not much to add here. Soooooo many families mistakenly think that they should not bother submitting financial aid applications. Sometimes they're right, many times they're dead wrong.

CHAPTER 3

WHAT INFORMATION GOES ON THE FORMS?

Your information!

Helpful, right?[19]

Fine. The real answer is that we'll spend a lot of time on this when I cover the financial aid formula, particularly your savings and assets. But I'm bringing up the following point because it's an important, nuanced point that bears emphasis:

There is a two-year "lookback" on FAFSA for INCOME, but...

Your ASSET information must be accurate *as of the date you file.*

If you're scratching your head, you have plenty of company. I get it all the time during my live, nonrefundable workshops[20] and webinars.

I'll put it another way: *there is no lookback for your savings information, but there IS a two-year lookback for your tax returns.*

---

[19] This is a good time to remind you that this book is nonrefundable.

[20] They're free but I think the "nonrefundable" joke is hilarious with repetition.

The Department Of Education refers to this as "Prior-Prior." So if you have a Class of 2020 graduate, your tax returns from 2018 are in play. If Class of 2021, your 2021 tax return counts. Get it?

That's the rule for INCOME.

Now, regarding ASSETS: As we'll discuss, you might be able to improve your eligibility for aid by "sheltering" your savings accounts, a/k/a moving money around[21] at the last minute.

Under these guidelines, you can shelter your savings accounts literally the day before you file your FAFSA and other forms. (Unlike Medicaid planning, where there is a five-year lookback to move assets out of an elderly parent's name to qualify for more health benefits. I really have no idea what I'm talking about here, so talk to an Elder Law attorney about this stuff - I'm a college guy, not a miracle worker, dammit Jim![22])

Of course you shouldn't wait until the last minute, any time you're faced with making financial decisions you should allow yourself plenty of time to understand the benefits AND costs.

_____

[21] Cliffhanger!

[22] That's a Star Trek reference, if you're keeping score at home.

CHAPTER 4

WHAT WILL YOU GET AFTER YOU APPLY?

How do colleges determine how much aid you'll qualify for? There are 70-plus factors that make up the key calculation in the financial aid formulas – the Expected Family Contribution (EFC). Here is an abbreviated, oversimplified explanation:

Income is the most heavily weighted factor – penalized between 22-47%. Fret not, I will explain what this means in a few short pages!

Assets are another factor – child savings are treated differently - i.e. penalized MUCH more severely - than parent assets (20% penalty versus 5.64%). Again, explanation forthcoming.

But these are not the only elements that can affect how much you'll have to pay for college. Here are a handful of other considerations:

- Your age
- The number of students in college at the same time
- Whether you own a business

- Your marital status[23]
- Things that have nothing to do with you, such as the historical generosity of the college and who else is applying

So just because you earn a decent income – or what you assume is a high salary – you should not blow off applying for financial aid. Income is but one of many factors.

Most financial aid applications are submitted in Fall of senior year. By March, your child will most likely have heard whether she was admitted to or denied from all colleges she applied to. (If you applied Early Decision, you hear back regarding admissions and financial aid/scholarships in December.)

A few weeks later, typically by the end of March, you will receive a financial aid award letter from each college your child has been admitted to.

What happens if you're not happy with the award? You can try to improve it, because it's not a firm, take it or leave it, written in stone award. It's only an OFFER.

You can try to improve your financial aid award letter – I cover this appeal process in a later chapter. Also (he said casually), I created a training class on all possible techniques you can use to

---

[23] "Status" means single or married, not "happy" or "I barely tolerate him."

improve a less-than-generous financial aid offer: www.AppealsClass.com .)[24]

Next, the dust settles, your child picks the college she'll attend and you're (moderately) happy with your financial aid award. Summer comes and goes and your child heads off to college.

Then he gets Straight A's, you re-apply for aid the following year, he founds and sells a company for a couple mill, marries a supermodel and runs for elective office. Or some version of that.

That's the financial aid process in a nutshell.

Now let's look at why college costs so much, so we can learn how to beat the greedy, overpriced rip-off colleges at their own game!

---

[24] There. There it is - my first sales pitch.

CHAPTER 5

COLLEGE TUITION IS "TOO DAMN HIGH!"

How can this be legal?

In 2010, this guy – I forget his name but remember the facial hair – ran for Governor of the State of New York under the auspices of the "Rent is Too Damn High" Party.

Mutton Chops cracked me up, but he had a point, easily transferable to the world of college costs: Tuition is too damn high! The odds are stacked against the average family.

I'm about to share something that stunned even me when I wrote the first edition of this magnificent tome. I'll let the numbers speak for themselves – annual cost of attendance from 2018, according to the College Board[25] by top private colleges:

College	Cost Of Attendance
Syracuse	$65,480
Boston University	$70,302
Boston College	$70,588
Northeastern	$68,537
Harvard	$69,510
Brown	$71,050
Dartmouth	$72,853
NYU	$72,900
University of Southern California	$72,277

---

[25] Who in no way endorses, approves of or wants anything to do with the author of this book. Sniff.

Notice anything odd about the numbers (other than how outrageously high they are)?

Isn't it weird how the prices are within a few bucks of each other. Hmmm.

Second, there isn't a round number anywhere, which isn't that meaningful but irritates me. Why can't Brown be $71,000, not $71,050?

Third, is there any valid reason why Harvard should be cheaper than BU or BC, etc.?

Or why Dartmouth should be more expensive than NYU, when you consider the cost of living in Hanover, New Hampshire versus downtown New York City?

Here are some more fun facts: College costs increase ALL the time – roughly double the rate of inflation[26]. Costs go up in good economies and bad economies.

Tuition and fees increase at roughly double the rate of inflation, and faster than every other benchmark, even health care costs.

No – something else is going on here.

Colleges are BUSINESSES (gasp!). Once you understand this, you can learn how to level the playing field.

---

[26] 1,000% in the last 30 years, vs. 300% inflation in the same period.

Like any business, they have expenses. And they must market themselves[27] to attract paying customers – what you and I call "college students."

Their goal – to get as much money out of your pockets as possible. You, of course, have the opposite goal – to spend as little as possible, perhaps doing something completely nuts like retiring someday, or paying off the mortgage.

If your child is shooting for a competitive college, but you're freaked out by these numbers (which do NOT include annual room and board, fees and other amounts totaling roughly $15,000 per school), I want you to know that the average discount given by a private college or university is more than 50%. (Feel better yet? A little?)

You need to understand one fundamental point: whether or not you realize it, YOU (and your kids) are in business for yourselves, too.

You're in the business of advocating for yourselves the best financial deal possible.

And your child is in the business of promoting him or herself to each college, explaining "THIS is why you should take me and

---

[27] Check your mailbox – ever wonder why you get emails, texts, calls and dozens of pieces of direct mail from colleges you never heard of each week?

give me boatloads of scholarships, compared to all of these other choices."

RESOURCE: If you want more information on what it REALLY takes to get into a top college, i.e. how to distinguish yourself from the other 5,000 competitor-applicants with the same grades and scores, you're invited to our next College Admissions "Secrets" webinar. It's free. The schedule is posted at: www.CollegeAdmissionsWebcast.com

Now, let's talk about about why it could be a deadly mistake to ask your guidance counselor, CPA or other "expert" about how to get money for college.

CHAPTER 6

WHY YOU SHOULDN'T ASK YOUR GUIDANCE COUNSELOR, THE FINANCIAL AID OFFICE OR YOUR ACCOUNTANT FOR HELP...

...unless you like banging your head against a brick wall

I'll comment on the whole guidance counselor thing in a minute, but let's start this discussion about those "friendly" offers to help from a college financial aid office.

In short, you've got a better shot of running into Michael Cohen, Esq.[28] at your next MENSA meeting than getting meaningful help from your assigned financial aid officer.

The reason is related to the nature of higher educational institutions themselves, as discussed in the previous chapter – they are BUSINESSES.

---

[28] Actually, "ex-Esq."

Yes, I know that colleges are ivory-towered institutions of higher education. However, they have bills to pay too, like any business. Here are a few line items on most schools' budgets:

"Deep" six or even seven figure salaries to pay to university presidents and other higher ups. And not only for colleges you've heard of, the president of Mountain State University earned $1.8 Million in 2009 (he was fired in 2012).

Many colleges employ marketing personnel to help them raise their profile and attract applicants. They don't come cheap: Most CMOs earn between $200,000-$400,000.

Upgrades to their already luxurious health facilities. Hey, you're slumming it if you don't have a rock climbing wall or "lazy river" for students to enjoy!

Dining options such as skirt steak, sushi, vegan, gluten-free and other fare required by today's teens. No more "Bug Juice" or "Mystery Meat."

Full-time wages for tenured professors who teach a grueling two classes per semester, which interferes with their research and publication of dry academic materials that no-one – even other academic types-will read.

Irony alert: Elizabeth Warren, Trump Arch Enemy and presidential hopeful Senator from Massachusetts, AND a self-described champion of college cost reform, taught one class at Harvard Law School in Fall 2011.

Her salary: $350,000.

Colleges are spending more on administrative staff than ever. According to a Bloomberg article, colleges employed 230,000 administrative staffers in 2009, up 60% since 1993, or 10 times the growth of teaching faculty.

The University of Connecticut's chief of police pulls in $256,000 per annum, more than New York City's police commissioner.

Also:

UConn has a $312,000-a-year provost and 13 vice, deputy and associate vice provosts, including one overseeing "engagement" who makes almost $275,000 a year. The university has seven vice presidents and 13 deans. President Susan Herbst, who receives a $500,000 salary, has a $199,000 chief of staff.

Don't ask a financial aid officer – an employee of this business – how to shave a few donuts off your bill. Asking the financial office for help is like calling the IRS and demanding that they reveal all their latest loopholes so you can lower your tax bill!

Your other choices:

High School guidance counselors: quality varies, just like doctors, lawyers and hair dressers. Even college consultants.

They can be great, they can be horrible (Note to any guidance counselors reading this – you're not one of the horrible ones![29]).

It's highly unusual to find a guidance counselor or college advisor, from a public or private high school, who understands the nuances buried in the 1,100-plus pages of the Title IV Federal Financial Aid regulations – which assets count against you more than others, which don't count against you at all, that kind of thing.

Parents complain how disappointed they are at their school's lack of financial guidance, but the problem is that they have unreasonable expectations. Guidance counselors aren't trained for this type of specialized knowledge, so it's unfair to expect them to have this expertise.

Not to mention their caseload – at many public schools one guidance counselor is in charge of 400 students, which is right around the national average (480:1, according to the last article I read). A huge chunk of their days is spent on endless meetings and other administrative tasks, dealing with scheduling, truancies, drug use, bullying, cyberbullying and other problems that your child may not have. Point is; there's not much time left over for individualized college advice about where to apply, what to major in, how to improve your odds of admission, let alone mastering college financial planning.

---

[29] And you're super-smart. Hey, have you lost weight?

Accountants and Financial Guys: Ditto for financial folks: CPA's, CFP's and other advisors rarely have more than a cursory understanding of the financial aid regulations, if they have any at all.

Truth be told, frequently, these advisors give advice that can flat-out slaughter your chances of qualifying for anything.

A common example: putting money in your child's name may, theoretically, help defer or reduce taxes (since earnings will be taxed at your child's lower rate) - but the financial aid formulas penalize child assets about four times as heavily as parent assets (20% versus 5.64%)!

Be careful who you listen to. By the time you make it through the end of this book, I bet you'll know more about financial aid than 99% of guidance counselors, accountants and other financial advisors. And you'll earn a hearty handshake from me![30]

RESOURCE: We cover the gory details about the financial aid process, soup-to-nuts, including key differences of the FAFSA and CSS Profile, in a free online workshop: www.FinancialAidWebcast.com

---

[30] Virtual handshake. We have a firm "no touch" rule at Lockwood College Prep., given the current political environment. #MeThree

CHAPTER 7

THE FINANCIAL AID "GAME" AND HOW TO WIN IT

Two near identical families. One does wicked awesome! The other…not so much

If you're like most parents of college-bound teens, you have a decent idea about how much college costs…but you're in the dark about how the financial aid "game" is played.

Maybe you've heard rumors of an apparently well-off family getting "a 100% free ride" for their kid, who wasn't an academic or athletic superstar.

How did they do this (putting aside the improbability that they actually received 100% funding)? It's possible that they were able to pay "wholesale" rates for college because they had the scuttlebutt on how to legally and ethically improve their eligibility.

As an analogy, I like the example of a senior citizen (usually an elderly parent), who hires an attorney to help him qualify for Medicaid (I always get "Medicaid" mixed up with "Medicare."

I'm pretty sure I mean Medicaid) in case he needs to go to a nursing home.[31]

In college financial aid planning, we don't use trusts or other legal instruments employed by Elder Law attorneys, and there's no five year "look back period," but the principles are the same – we shelter assets to improve eligibility for benefits.

Note how your eligibility may be unaffected by how much money you've saved. Because if you've stashed your money, in the "wrong" places, you might be able to re-allocate your assets into "buckets" that penalize you less severely, or don't penalize you at all.

Example: Family A and Family B[32] can have substantially the same amount of income, assets, home equity, children and so forth, for example:

Adjusted Gross Income	$150,000
No. children:	3
College funds	$200,000
Home value	$800,000
Mortgage Balance	$300,000
Retirement Savings	$400,000

---

[31] The "Medicaid Spend down."

[32] Their real names.

Children from each family apply to the exact same schools, but Family A will end up paying full price, possibly taking on large amounts of college debt that will haunt them and their children for years.

Family B, on the other hand, will send their children to the same colleges for a 25-30% (or more) discount, reducing or avoiding their reliance on pricey student loan debt to pay for college.

The Wall Street Journal put it best – "It's not how much money you've saved, it's where you've saved that money."[33]

Now let's drill down on how the financial aid office calculates how much – or how little – financial aid it will award.

---

[33] Reprinted withOUT permission

CHAPTER 8

EFC AND THE "DOUBLE-SECRET" FORMULA

The Department of Education has its own particular way of calculating how much you can afford to pay for college. Its rules are followed by most colleges in the country.

Yup. Just fill out the FAFSA, hit the "submit" button and Presto! out spits your Expected Family Contribution, otherwise known as EFC.

That number represents the amount of money that the government, in all of its wisdom and glory, thinks you can afford to pay for one year of higher education. NOT necessarily what you will pay, but what you appear to be able to afford under the formulas, known as the "Federal Methodology."

Factors include: income, number of family members in college, assets of the parent, assets of the child and more.

Wondering what your EFC is? I'll tell you how to estimate it – in a minute.

WARNING – you will probably be very angry, shocked, confused or depressed by your EFC. Or, think it's a cruel joke.

Why? The average EFC for a family earning $120,000 in adjusted gross income is roughly $35,000.

You read that correctly – a family earning a low six-figure income – before paying income taxes, property taxes, the mortgage and all of the other expenses associated with modern life– is expected to be able to pay $35,000 per year toward college.

The biggest flaw in the EFC formula is that it doesn't factor expenses. So if you live in an expensive area of the country, like a suburb in the Northeast, and you earned $120,000, your EFC would be identical to a family with the same financial profile living in Sheboygan, Wisconsin, where the cost of living might be 50% less!

The good news is that you can control your EFC, with planning.

I'm no psychic, but I predict that, after you calculate your EFC, you are going to be very interested in learning how to lower it.

The Department of Education helps you estimate your EFC:here's where to go:

http://www.fafsa4caster.ed.gov

Also, each college publishes a Net Price Calculator on its website. They are a good starting point, but not 100% reliable, for a variety of reasons, including the old "Garbage in, garbage out," a/k/a "user error" issue, AND that there is no uniform set of criteria required by each calculator - some ask for more data than others.

I encourage you to think of the FAFSA Forecaster and Net Price Calculators as good starting points.

> RESOURCE: After you calculate your EFC and you've had sufficient time to sulk, watch our free online class to learn how to lower your EFC (and improve your eligibility for need-based aid): www.FinancialAidWebcast.com

The Institutional Methodology

Approximately 400 private colleges use the CSS Profile to calculate your EFC a different way, using what's called the "Institutional Methodology."[34]

One of the key differences between the Federal Methodology, used by FAFSA-only colleges, and the Institutional Methodology is that the **Institutional Methodology factors in the equity you appear to have in your home** (the difference between the fair market value of your home and your mortgage balances), reasoning that if you have it, you'll use it by pulling a home equity line of credit (compared to a high rate, high fee parent loan or private student loan).

---

[34] This term is a misnomer, since there is no published formula pertaining to the Institutional Methodology, the way there is with the "Federal Methodology."

There are exceptions. Harvard's website is very clear that it does NOT count home equity against you, for example (with an endowment valued at more than $30 Billion, Harvard probably won't lose sleep over giving you a few extra bucks).

Stanford and Hamilton are two other colleges that don't penalize you for owning a home.

Duke counts only a certain portion of the apparently available equity, not every last dollar. Example: if your fair market value is $750,000, but you owe $150,000, most CSS Profile schools would penalize you on the $600,000 (750K value less 150K owed). But Duke, and a handful of other CSS Profile colleges, cap the penalty on home equity based on income level.[35]

My back of the napkin way to calculate EFC for a private school is to use the FAFSA Forecaster link above, then add $5,000 for every $100,000 (5%) of home equity (fair market value of your home less any mortgage balances).

So if your FAFSA forecaster EFC is $30,000 and you have $200,000 in home equity, your Institutional Methodology EFC could be around $40,000: $30,000 FAFSA EFC plus the $10,000 penalty on equity (5% of 200,000)[36].

---

[35] Your head hurt yet? To make things more complicated, Duke says it penalizes up to 8% of parent assets, when the Federal Methodology says 5.64%.

[36] Math Whiz Andy Lockwood!

Since October 2011, the Department of Education has required colleges to post a Net Price Calculator on their respective websites, as previously mentioned. Although potentially misleading (there's no standardized set of information they must ask), it's worth doing, because it helps families see that they may not have to pay "Sticker Price" for college.

Here's the link to the College Board's Net Price Calculator. Play around with it but don't rely 100% on it.[37]

http://netpricecalculator.collegeboard.org/

Let's take a closer look at how colleges use your EFC.

---

[37] Don't rely on it either way. A few weeks ago, a client received from Washington & Lee $10,000 more than what the Net Price Calculator estimated. That was fun!

CHAPTER 8

THE "DOUBLE-SECRET" FORMULA IN ACTION

How to determine how much – or little – financial aid you'll get

Now, a quick (read, "oversimplified") lesson on the formula used by each school to determine your financial aid award. Here it is:

COA   Cost Of Attendance

-EFC   Expected Family Contribution

=NEED   Financial Need

"Cost of Attendance" means one year of tuition, fees, room and board, etc.

Expected Family Contribution is a formulaic number that indicates how much you can afford to pay for one year of college, according to the Department of Education. (Calculated automatically after you file the FAFSA – the Free Application for Financial Aid.)

Need. Schools award financial aid based on how much need you show. Once you identify the percentage of need that your college meets, you have a decent handle on what your award will look like by plugging that data into the formula. Here is a simplified example:

COA	$60,000
-EFC	$30,000
=NEED	$30,000

You pay your EFC plus any unmet need.

Scenario 1: 100% of Need Met

If a college meets 100% of need, you pay your EFC of $30,000 only. In other words, you cover what the formula "expects" you to cover and the college will foot the bill for the rest.

Generally, the most elite, competitive colleges in the country will meet 100% of need. I listed them at the end of this masterpiece, somewhere around page 785.[38] Most schools do not meet 100% of need, however. (Spoiler alert.)

Scenario 2: 90% Need Met

EFC + Unmet Need

If the college meets 90% of need, you'll pay your EFC of $30,000 PLUS the unmet need, or $3,000, calculated as follows:

---

[38] Hah. Had you going for a moment. But I do list them later.

90% of total ($30,000) need is $27,000 ($30,000 x .90).

In other words, you'll pay:

EFC + Unmet Need

$30,000 (EFC) + $3,000 (Unmet need) = $33,000

Make sense?

Scenario 3. 75% of Need Met

A college could meet only 75% of need, or $22,500. You can do the arithmetic on this one - give it a go, Sparky![39]

Fine, I'll do it.

EFC + Unmet Need

$30,0000 + $7,500 = $37,500.

How can you obtain information about school generosity? Look on the websites for each college – specifically, for its Net Price Calculators. (You may have to click around for a while – colleges don't make this info easy to find.) You can also call the financial aid office but you'll probably end up frustrated by the lack of responsiveness, according to most of the parents I work with.

Another great resource is the Common Data Set – a clearinghouse of data self-reported by colleges. Warning: you'll see a TON of

---

[39] Do not let condescending nicknames like this prevent you from giving this book a 5 star rating it deserves.

information, which can be overwhelming. Nonetheless, almost everything you'd want to know about paying for college is buried somewhere:

Percentage of financial need met

What percentage of the average award is free (grants) versus loans and work study,

Average award for freshmen vs. all undergraduate students

Graduation rates and

A lot (a lot!) more.

If you're the analytical, roll up your sleeves and dig in to the data type of guy/gal, the Common Data Set will be like Disney World[40] for you!

No matter whether you seek help or do it yourself, preparation and research can pay off in a big way.

Conversely, blowing it off could cost tens of thousands of dollars in financial aid that was yours for the taking. That's bad.

Next we'll look at some juicy loopholes that could boost your eligibility!

---

[40] Without the unavoidable gift shop standing between the end of every ride and the exit.

CHAPTER 9

SOME "STUFF" COUNTS AGAINST YOU MORE THAN OTHERS…SOME NOT AT ALL!

Deciphering the twisted, counter-intuitive Financial Aid Regulations

Here's where it gets complicated. But it's also where the opportunities lay, so listen up!

In summary:

"Kid stuff" – assets and income – count against you more than "parent stuff."

Here's a simplified chart:

	Income	*Assets*
Parent	22-47	5
Child	50	20-25

Skip the income column for a moment. In the formulas, parent assets are penalized between 5.64% and 12%[41]. In other words, $100,000 of parent money will gross up your EFC - reduce your eligibility – by a minimum of $5,000 and change.

However: If you held that same $100,000 in your child's name, your EFC would increase by 20% or 25%.[42]

In other words, your EFC penalty would be $20,000 or $25,000!

Yes, that's per year.

By contrast, if I took that 100G's and went to Vegas (I'm soooooo "money"), I'd be eligible for $20,000-$25,000 more financial aid per year than you, because my questionable behavior removed that asset from my financial aid balance sheet. I'm rewarded for being irresponsible!

Not to get political, this amounts to a penalty for doing the right thing – saving money for your child.

(Awkward silence.)

---

[41] From the "Too Geeky to Matter" Department: it's really 5.64%, having to do with how the formulas convert assets to income. And some schools – Duke is one of them – penalize 8%. Some parents say they've heard 12%. But hear me now and believe me later - just use 5%!

[42] This depends on the college. Some private colleges assess a 25% penalty, most private and all public use 20%.

Speaking of disincentives, student income is penalized more severely than parent income. The parent income penalty is between 22-47% on a sliding scale, and a large chunk is excluded (this is known as the "Income Protection Allowance").

On the other hand, student income gets dinged 50% from the get-go – there's no excluded amount.

A "Cray-Cray" Example

Check this out – if your kid is hard working enough to earn $10,000 and save it, he'll pay:

- Income taxes on the earnings
- A 50% financial aid "penalty" on the earnings, and
- A 20% penalty on the money he stuck in his savings account (25% at some schools)

So he'll net $1,000-$1,500 if he's lucky! He'd be better off sitting out, not working.[43]

Bad Advice On Where To Save

Back to savings accounts and the advice that your well-intentioned CPA or "Wealth Manager" gave you to set up child savings accounts – UGMA's, UTMA's, typically. He told you to do this because of the tax benefits (lower rates, you withdraw money without penalty), but that advice will bite you in the tush!

---

[43] Calling John Galt! Oops, guess I got political.

It could disqualify you for grants, scholarships and other financial aid because your penalty is 20% instead of the 5.64% you'd pay if you kept the funds in your own name.

Or zero if you sheltered it in an exempt asset, which I cover in the next chapter![44]

529 College Savings Accounts

Under the Federal rules, 529 accounts are parent assets, meaning they are penalized at a lower rate (they used to be considered a child asset until Congress changed things in 2006) instead of 20% for a child asset.

Any 529 owned by a parent, naming the child as the beneficiary, is a parent asset on the FAFSA.

What about 529's owned by a grandparent, naming the child as a beneficiary?

NOT an asset reported on the FAFSA! But before you call up Grandma, here are two caveats:

1. When Grandma withdraws 529 funds to pay for college, FAFSA treats that amount as INCOME to the child. In other words, it levies a stiff 50% penalty on those funds. Example: Grandma sends $20K to college. The following year, College Boy is penalized $10,000, 50% of the amount Grandma sent.

---

[44] a/k/a "The Meat Of This Book" (finally)

So try to delay using the grandparent 529 until after your last FAFSA is filed, or junior year of college.

2.   So far, this discussion pertains to FAFSA only.   In my experience (and that of my colleagues in other parts of the country), many private colleges and universities that use the CSS Profile will treat the 529 as a child asset and reduce your eligibility sharply (by 20-25%).

What do you do if you have a 529?

It may pay to sell it early, but understand that you will pay a penalty if you do not use the funds for "Qualified Higher Education Expenses" (tuition, books, room and board) if attending at least half-time. The penalty is 10% of the earnings on the 529. (Good news/bad news: earnings haven't been all that great lately. The penalty may not be terrible, it depends on your "cost basis" – what you invested.)

If you received a deduction for investing in the 529 (some states give you one), you may have to "recapture" your deduction, meaning reverse it.   Work through this stuff with someone competent before you start moving your 529's willy-nilly.

Trusts

Occasionally, parents ask me whether trusts are a good idea for college financial aid planning. The answer is usually no. Trusts naming kids as beneficiaries are not exempt, they count. The "corpus," or assets held by the trust, are penalized at the child rate.

Practically all trusts allow the trustee to use funds to pay for the child's education, so this treatment in the financial aid regulations makes sense. However, in the case where the trust restricts the child's access to the funds until a certain age, like 21 or 30, you may succeed in an argument to the financial aid office that the trust assets should not be considered as resources that can be used to pay for college (if that's truly how the trust documents read).

Financial aid officers have "Professional Judgment," or discretion, to consider the story beyond the proverbial four corners of the financial aid forms (more on this topic later).

Next, we'll look at exempt assets – savings that don't count against you at all!

CHAPTER 10

EXEMPT ASSETS

"Loopholes" that could multiply your eligibility

The legal department (OK, me – I'm on a budget and Dershowitz won't return my calls) warned me to issue this weasel-like, lawyerly disclaimer:

Nothing in this chapter or book is meant as LEGAL ADVICE.

Neither is it FINANCIAL ADVICE. I am not a licensed stockbroker, insurance agent, accountant, mortician or cosmologist.[45] And even if it works for financial aid purposes, it may not be suitable for financial PLANNING purposes.

In other words, advice may work in terms of improving eligibility for financial aid, but you'd better consider carefully the legal, tax and all other non-financial aid implications. Talk to a qualified professional advisor about this stuff.

Last, a note on lying on the forms:

Don't lie.

---

[45] Although I did serve as in-house counsel to a publicly traded brokerage company in Miami, back in the 90's. And I am a licensed Mixologist.

Seriously, do you need me to tell you this? (AHEM, cough cough, Felicity. Lori.)

If the FAFSA asks about cash, don't "forget" about what's under your proverbial mattress.

If you have money in CDs or savings accounts that you forget about on the forms, it will catch up to you once the financial aid office sees the interest and/or dividends on your tax returns.

Let's talk liability. Everyone knows that people who lie on the FAFSA don't go to heaven.

Second, the penalties for fraud on the FAFSA include stiff fines (10 G's) and jail time. So you AND your kid could each go away next year!

She'll have a normal roommate at college, yours will be named "Bubba" up at the Big House.

Schools have gotten better at detecting fraud, too. And more aggressive about requesting "Verification" on financial aid forms when a red flag (inconsistent answers, mostly) triggers heightened scrutiny. Extra scrutiny rarely results in an increased award, by the by.

Enough double-talk! Let's look at five classes of assets that are exempt in the financial aid formulas.

1. Retirement Accounts

2. Annuities

3. Insurance with cash value

4. Primary residence (FAFSA schools only)

5. Business Assets

Here are my comments on each:

Retirement Accounts.

Under the Federal rules, the value of your retirement accounts (401K, 403B, 457, IRA, SEP, SIMPLE, etc.) is not considered an "investment" and should not be included as a parent asset. They don't count against you.

On the other hand, if you *mistakenly* disclose any of these types of savings, you will have shot yourself in the foot. If this happened, you have plenty of company. Plenty of smart, paperwork-savvy folks make this mistake and others like it all the time.

If you goofed up this way, please put this book down, log into your FAFSA and correct this mistake immediately. Then notify each college on your list of what transpired.[46]

But here's a little twisteroo on the whole retirement thang:

---

[46] Then go to Amazon and give this book a 5 star rating and glowing review.

Any contributions you make to your retirement account in the "Base Year" (the tax year ending two years before the academic year – if your student graduates high school in Fall 2021, the base year is 2019) count as *income!*

In other words, if you lowered your Adjusted Gross Income by $15,000 because of your retirement contribution – from $165,000 down to $150,000 – FAFSA considers your income to be $165,000, and will penalize you about 47% of that increase – almost $8,000.

So the asset is exempt, but the act of contributing to the account isn't. Stupid, right?

Perhaps. I suppose the feds don't want us to double dip, benefitting both from a tax deduction AND two financial aid benefits.

On the other hand, if there's a public policy behind the rules along the lines of "Parents shouldn't have to rob their retirement savings to pay for college," why is the ACT of saving that money penalized?[47]

Despite this screwy financial aid issue, you'll never hear me advise anyone to stop funding their IRA or 401K, because you can never have enough retirement savings. But do so with your eyes wide open about the implications.

---

[47] Rhetorical question. Don't answer, just stew about it angrily like me.

Annuities

Annuities are exempt under the FAFSA, meaning that any annuities that you own will not count as "investments" under the Federal rules. (And that if you mistakenly *include* them on the FAFSA you will die a prolonged, miserable death.)[48] But there are a couple of issues that I want to call to your attention.

Several years back, I was conducting a workshop in Oyster Bay, Long Island, when a guy raised his hand as I was discussing annuities.

"I have paperwork at home, I'm about to buy an annuity that another college planner sold me," he said.

> Sidebar: Many "college planners" are licensed financial advisors e.g. stockbrokers, insurance guys. I believe that most do their business in an ethical way, but a fraction of them are a little sneaky. They conduct college planning seminars, get clients to hire them, advise that they can improve their eligibility by "shifting" their cash into a financial product, then mention, "Oh, and by the way, I sell annuities! What a coincidence! And I have an application right here in my jacket! Egad![49] Another coincidence!"

---

[48] Which, ironically, might feel the same as reading this book!

[49] What's wrong with "Egad!"?

But this was not the main problem. I asked, "What colleges are on your list?"

The guy rattled off 10-11 colleges, all but two required the CSS Profile.

The issue: annuities are NOT completely exempt as shelters on this form. Put another way, the only person likely to benefit from the annuity purchase was the insurance salesman/college planner!

Giving him the benefit of the doubt, the insurance salesman may have known that annuities were legitimate shelters on the FAFSA, but didn't understand that they don't work for CSS Profile colleges.

Turns about my workshop attendee was prepared to invest several hundred thousand dollars, which is why his insurance guy now has my photo on a dartboard somewhere.

Insurance

Cash value life insurance products are exempt on the FAFSA and CSS Profile.[50] Each year, I personally advise a select number of

---

[50] Although at least two colleges ask whether you have insurance via their supplemental financial aid forms.

families improve their eligibility by moving money into a cash value life insurance policy.

A word of caution: be certain that you understand the benefits - and potential negatives – of investing in these instruments.

Specifically, look at the fees and make certain you understand the restrictions and penalties associated with accessing your money ("surrender charges") BEFORE you sign.

One of my favorite sayings is "Man plans and God laughs,"[51] which I first heard from a client who was born in a concentration camp in Poland.

In the context of this discussion,[52] the point is that you may decide to make a move after you've evaluated all the pros and cons, but your assumptions at the time of your decision may be flawed – life has a funny way of serving up unexpected stuff.

How much would it suck to go back to your broker a year later, tell him you need to get more money than you originally anticipated, only to learn that you'll pay a $12,000 surrender charge to withdraw your funds?

---

[51] "Der mentsh trakht un got lakht" in Yiddish, if you must know.

[52] As opposed to an existential "meaning of life" debate. This is a financial aid book.

I recommend that to leave yourself a lot more access ("liquidity") than you think you need, even if it hurts a smidgen in financial aid eligibility.

Your primary residence.

FAFSA specifically excludes the value of your primary residence (note – investment properties and second homes ARE assets). Occasionally, people ask me whether they should shelter cash by paying off their mortgage.

As a recovering debt-laden person, I love getting this question and the mentality of the person asking. But this may not be the best idea for two reasons.

1. Colleges requiring the CSS Profile treat the primary residence as a potential resource to pay for college (e.g. pulling out a home equity line of credit), and

2. "Man plans, God laughs." I don't like the idea of tying up money in a home, then trying to get it out by borrowing when something unforeseen happens.

First, you're paying interest on money that was interest-free in the recent past.

Second, you may not be able to get it! After the 2008 mortgage meltdown, banks froze access to equity lines, cut them, and wiped them out completely in some cases. Could there be *another* financial crisis that causes banks to shut down equity lines and other panicky moves?

Of course not, that would be crazy, right?[53]

Mark Twain's famous (non-Yiddish) quote goes something like, "A banker is a fellow who lends you his umbrella when the sun is shining, but wants it back the minute it begins to rain."

In other words, the best time to ask for money is when you do NOT need it.

Let's say you lose your job, then go to the bank for a loan to help you pay your bills. The underwriters care about your ability to pay them back more than anything else, so you're 99% certain to be denied at that point. Even if you have NO mortgage on your home and a perfect credit score, it's tough – the lending guidelines have changed since 2008, big league!

Neither I nor any self-proclaimed "schmexpert" can predict what's going to happen in the future.[54]

Strategic Equity Management

Here is one more strategy that is definitely NOT for most folks – frankly, it's a little scary.

---

[53] Note the sarcasm. Draw your own conclusions.

[54] Except that Bitcoin will be worth more than $100,000 after you finish this book.

Sometimes people pull money out of their home (by taking an equity line or remortgaging) and stash it in an exempt asset. The theory[55] is that, since CSS Profile colleges will treat the apparent equity in your home as a resource you can use to pay for college, you might as well be proactive about doing so on your own terms, not those of the college financial aid office, in a way that will not count against you.

Before I get to the negatives (they are significant), let me flesh out the positive.

My client, Seth (not his real name) owned a home worth 750,000 with a mortgage of 175,000. Seth's[56] two boys were considering colleges like Boston College, MIT, Middlebury, Fairfield, Loyola University Maryland and other private schools.

Each is a CSS Profile school that counts home equity as an asset.

Seth is self-employed, and, thanks to his accountant, shows a low, six-figure income on paper. Between his apparent home equity and other savings, Seth's total includable assets were close to $800,000.

In the financial aid formulas, that $800,000 equates to a penalty of approximately $44,500. An *annual* decrease in eligibility of 44 Large.

---

[55] Created by a mortgage broker (surprise!)

[56] His real name is Ralph.

Put another way, by sheltering these assets, Seth could improve his eligibility for financial aid (mostly free money from the schools on his boys' lists) by up to $44,500, per year.

Seth took a larger mortgage, which decreased his equity. Luckily, by remortgaging, Seth was able to reduce his interest rate and term significantly, so his payments increased only $200 per month, so there was no issue with affording the payments.

Next, Seth moved a chunk of his assets into his business account as a loan (strategy described in the next chapter).

Note that Seth *didn't consume his home equity*, instead he pulled it out of his home, where it was "trapped in the bricks," then placed it into another safe, liquid investment. And he could make the payments, no sweat.

Several stars had to align for this strategy to make sense:

1. Seth had to be able to afford the new payments

2. He had to avoid doing something dumb with the proceeds from the refinance (e.g. getting jet skis for everyone, buying another property that could lose value and tie up cash)

3. He needed reasonable certainty that at least one of his kids would end up at a private college that penalized him for having equity.

When I first wrote this section, I started twitching from nerves because I was imagining thousands of readers[57] recklessly pulling equity out of their homes and flushing the money down the toilet.

But I trust you to evaluate this technique from all angles and using common sense. In Seth's case, it worked out: each of the colleges his boys ended up at gave substantial awards, so Seth was able to comfortably afford to send them to their top choice colleges.

OK, one more tip about how to reduce home value: when Pearl[58] does the CSS Profiles for our clients, she frequently compares the value of the home the client gives against a Department of Commerce methodology known as the "Federal Housing Index Multiplier."

The Multiplier asks for two bits of information: when you bought your home and the purchase price. Then it calculates a value based on national averages, which in many cases is lower because the rate of appreciation across the country is typically less than areas like Long Island, Connecticut and other suburban areas where our clients tend to live.

Many homeowners wonder whether they can use the assessed value (as given by their county tax assessor) to calculate value. You cannot.

---

[57] Or, six.

[58] My "little lady," who handles financial aid form preparation in the office (she does the real work).

Assessed value is typically lower than the true fair market value that you could sell your home for. That's why all financial aid offices tell you not to use it. The directions on the FAFSA and CSS Profile tell you assessed value cannot be used also.

Bottom line – value is in the eye of the beholder. The Multiplier technique is not failsafe but it tends to work most of the time if you've owned your home for more than five years and live in an area of the country where homes have appreciated faster than average (near metropolitan areas, generally). CSS Profile colleges usually calculate your home value by a method similar to the federal Multiplier, so it's worth a shot, and, if the financial aid office gives you grief, you can show a reasonable, third party basis for arriving at your value.

RESOURCE: To see the formulas in "action" (that's a stretch) enroll in a free online workshop at www.FinancialAidWebcast.com

CHAPTER 11

THE ULTIMATE SMALL BUSINESS LOOPHOLE

FAFSA asks self-employed people to value their business. The directions are explicit, but often overlooked, even by the best and brightest financial minds, because they're buried.

Even if you're not self-employed, I'm pretty sure you'd stipulate that there are multiple ways to value a business – one way if you're selling, another if you're filing taxes – you get the point. All legal.

More than 10 years ago, I was discussing this in a workshop in Parkland, Florida. I asked whether anyone there was self-employed. A guy in a nice, pinstriped suit[59] raised his hand.

"What do you do?"

"I'm a CPA."

Crap, I thought. *This guy's going to argue with me about all the tax stuff...* But, being the brave, mature professional that I am, I asked him how he would value his business.

---

[59] Unusual for Florida!

Before answering, the bean counter told me that he had, in fact, done the FAFSA the previous year, his daughter was at Barnard, and other "backstory" facts he felt I the rest of the people in the room needed to know, like how great her grades were and what other schools wanted her.[60]

"OK," I said, "don't tell me the number, but tell me HOW you arrived at the value of your business."

"Well, firms like mine are valued at 1.5 times book, we have receivables, we own our building, have a mortgage..."

He was in the middle of rendering a very CPA-like, or banker-like, answer.

"How many employees do you have?" I interrupted.

"It varies – during tax season we bring in extras because we're so busy...14 employees total," he said, straightening up in his chair, looking around, clearly proud of his bustling enterprise.

"OK. I understand your answer, and I'm not arguing. But for FAFSA purposes, your business is worth zero," I replied.

"What? It is NOT! I got two offers this year alone to be bought out for a great multiple!" he sputtered.

I get it. It's tough being in business. Sometimes it feels like the world is against you – employees who need babysitting, clients

---

[60] You'd be shocked at how often this happens at live workshops. Unless I just described your behavior.

who don't pay, dumb regulations and taxes, long hours. Mental toughness is critical for business owners.

But for financial aid purposes, you've got to think strategically. Check your ego and emotions at the door. On paper, think doom and gloom - be negative! In the bizarre world of FAFSA rules, looking "bad" means you'll get good results.

My new friend was miffed when I told him that his oversight "lost" him $8,000-10,000 in aid from Barnard. What was the mistake?

FAFSA rules say that any family-owned business that employs fewer than 100 employees has a zero value. Are your wheels turning?

I have a client, Stacy, who owns a small, minority-owned business – a marketing agency. Through an inheritance, she had a stock portfolio of about $650,000, and her daughter was getting ready to apply to a highly-ranked, Jesuit institution on the East Coast.[61]

Stacy and her husband's income was low on paper, but their portfolio alone would penalize them at least $36,000 in lost eligibility.

After conferring with her CPA, Stacy loaned her business the entire amount, which she accomplished without selling or buying any securities, which could have triggered gains that would flow

---

[61] Which rhymes with "Nilla-nova."

through to her tax return, in effect, removing the assets from her personal balance sheet.

The result: hefty, $30,000-plus awards each year.

Another client, Tina, owns a construction business with her husband in our neighborhood. She did the FAFSA and CSS Profile herself for her older daughter, who was admitted to NYU, Syracuse and other expensive, private colleges.

Her offer? Zilch, across the board. Total whiff.

She retained me to take a look at her forms. I noticed her mistake almost immediately: she used a *real world* value for her business pulled from her audited financial statements she's required to submit to her company's equipment lenders.

But Tina employed 18 people, so her business is worth zero too.

Pearl corrected this mistake and quickly refiled, and we dashed off a letter of explanation.

NYU sent back a revised offer: $25,000!

That was three years ago, she received the same award each of the next two years also, now she is $75,000 to the positive. Not too shabby!

You may wonder, "What about schools that take the CSS Profile?" Tina's and Stacy's daughter attends one of these colleges.

The CSS Profile requires business owners to divulge additional information about their business via an extra form, the Business/Farm Supplement. This form asks for the equivalent of a P&L (Profit and Loss statement) and a Balance Sheet for the current and previous years.

The main part of the CSS Profile will ask you the value of your business and number of employees.

So if business assets get disclosed on the CSS Profile, why did this strategy work for Stacy, Tina and other business owners?

My guess is that it has to do with how the forms look. Actually, the psychology of how they're READ. On one hand, the FAFSA and CSS Profile are very "official" looking documents – together – almost 30 pages of typed, neatly presented information.

The Business/Farm Supplement, on the other hand, is handwritten by the applicant's accountant, and faxed and re-faxed a few times. It's messy. Viscerally, it's the less important-looking form.

Also, financial aid officers aren't necessarily investment bankers or business valuation experts, they may not know how to read a financial statement like a business owner might.

But under the Institutional Methodology, business assets factor into the calculation of net worth. I'm told that financial aid officers at CSS Profile colleges "haircut" or minimize their impact, on purpose or by default.

Get a job, kid

Other of my "pet" strategies for business owners include putting their children on payroll (they're taxed at a lower rate), and/or implementing Tuition Benefit Plans to pay for employees of the business, establishing IRAs for their children.

A full discussion is beyond the scope of this chapter, but business owners would be well-served to consult an expert on these college funding strategies for business owners. Start with your own accountant.

If he or she is not clear how the Treasury Department IRS rules jibe with the Department of Education Title IV regulations, you may want to add a college funding expert to your team.[62]

---

[62] Preferably one at least 6'2", a best selling author and who giggles uncontrollably at his own jokes.

CHAPTER 12

SEVENTEEN COSTLY FAFSA MISTAKES TO AVOID

Like A Toothbrush in a Gas Station Bathroom

Let's take a quick break and review a short list of the most common mistakes I see when I'm reviewing previously filed financial aid forms for prospective clients. Pay attention, committing any of these mistakes boosts your EFC and costs you thousands – even tens of thousands – of dollars in "lost" financial aid eligibility!

This chapter alone is worth the price of your nonrefundable book, many, many times over![63]

1. Mixing student "stuff" up with parent "stuff." FAFSA's sections switch back and forth between child and parent info. Child assets "count" against you much more than parent assets – roughly 20% compared to 5.64%. (So if your child has $100,000 in her name your EFC will increase by $20,000. That same amount treated as a parent asset results in a boost of your EFC to only $5,640.) Double and triple check your work!

---

[63] Starting to annoy myself with the repetition.

74

2. Disclosing the value of your retirement accounts (401K, 403B, 457, IRA, SEP, SIMPLE, etc.). FAFSA directions very clearly tell you NOT to include retirement accounts.

3. Disclosing the value of life insurance and annuities. FAFSA directions tell you not to include these either.

4. Including the value of your home when you answer the question about your investments. The directions tell you to exclude the value of your primary residence. NOTE – you must include values of investment properties.

5. Not indicating that you want to be considered for work study and loans. Check this box, even if you plan not to take loans or work. You're not obligating yourself, when and if you're offered these types of aid, you can refuse the offer. Say "yes" to show the financial aid office that you need money, make your final decision to accept or not, later.

6. Waiting until you've completed your tax returns before tackling the FAFSA. The FAFSA comes out in October. Many schools have priority deadlines of February 1st, February 15th and March 1st (check with each school on your list).

Thanks to a rule change in 2016, you will be able to submit the FAFSA with information from your tax return from two years earlier. (Example: if your child graduates 2019, you can now port in your IRS info from 2017 via the "IRS Data Retrieval Tool."[64]

7. Blowing Priority Deadlines. Many schools award money on a first come, first-served basis. Typically, all financial aid applications received before the deadline are considered equally, whether they were filed weeks or hours before.

Please make sure you check two deadlines for each college on your list: the ADMISSIONS application deadline, and the PRIORITY financial aid deadline!

8. Making careless typographical mistakes – transposing digits of a social security number, date of birth, confusing parent and child dates of birth, social security numbers and so forth. Sometimes social security numbers are incorrect on tax returns, because CPAs are human too! These gaffes have nothing to do with the substance of your application (income, assets, etc.), but they can cause delays in processing your FAFSA – maybe two-three weeks of lost time that can cause you to miss out on the "good" aid by the time your application gets back up in the queue.

9. Over-valuing your business if you're self-employed. A close look at the directions tells you that business assets are exempt if

---

[64] The IRS DRT works MOST of the time. 2017 was dicey, the tool worked, then it shut down, then it worked again. Hopefully by the time you read this it will be fine. No promises.

you employ fewer than 100 employees. Big loophole! (See previous chapter.)

10. Not filing. I've seen it more than once, people slog through the form, think they're done, and log out. But it ain't over 'til it's over – the FAFSA must be "signed" electronically (via a signature involving your FSA ID) and submitted. The FAFSA walks you through exactly how to do this, so no excuses - colleges don't get your form until you hit the submit button!

11. Messing up the tax information: confusing adjusted gross income, reporting taxes withheld from your paycheck (instead of total taxes paid- they're different numbers) and other related errors.

12. Using a nickname instead of a given name ("Jimmy" instead of "James.")[65]. FAFSA may not be able to match a nickname with the social security number.

13. In the case of a divorced family, using the info for the *incorrect* parent. ("Incorrect" means less advantageous under the financial aid rules, not an ex-spouse who's always wrong.)

FAFSA's directions indicate that you should use the parent with whom the child spent the majority – more than half – of his or her

---

[65] Or "Slim Smoove Shady Man" instead of, "Harold."

time. (Note: that this is an entirely different issue than which parent declares the child as a dependent on his/her tax returns.[66]

14. Not catching mistakes on the Student Aid Report (SAR), which the Department of Education sends you a few days after you file the FAFSA. If a number is transposed, a date of birth incorrect, etc. this is another chance to catch it. Correct it immediately!

15. Failure to be consistent with the CSS Profile and other forms. Don't give the financial aid officer any reason to doubt your numbers, they check the forms for consistency.

16. Not filing at all for any reason. 53% of all eligible families don't even bother to file, according to one study that I see on the Internet all the time, so it must be true.

Hockey great Wayne Gretzky is credited with the quote, "You miss 100% of the shots you don't take." Don't leave any money on the table, don't blow off filing just because you think you earn too much or someone says "That school won't give you anything!"

17. Listing some, not all of the colleges you're applying to, on the FAFSA You send the FAFSA to each school you want to

---

[66] In many cases, divorced parents take turns claiming the child as a dependent for the tax year. So a kid can be a dependent of the mother in Year One, and the father in Year Two. But for financial aid purposes, the mom could be the custodial parent for each of Year One and Two without it being inconsistent on your tax returns.

consider giving you money. Don't leave off any college you or your child is applying to!

Here's a common mistake: if your kid decides to apply to a few more colleges after the initial wave of applications goes in, you must be diligent about updating FAFSA, CSS Profile, too. It does NOT happen automatically.

18. Failure to follow up with the financial aid office after you file, to ensure they received everything. I know, you have a printed receipt from FAFSA indicating which schools got the form, but sometimes colleges can't find your silly old FAFSA!

Or, more common, you filed it, you have your receipt but the college sends you an urgent email, WE DON'T HAVE YOUR FAFSA! YOU'LL GET NOTHING AND LIKE IT!"

Don't panic, just show them your receipt and resend, if necessary.

Don't assume anything – make sure you follow up!

Confused? Don't be. Join us for our next webcast, the *"Dirty Little Secrets" Of FAFSA, Financial Aid & Scholarships:* www.FinancialAidWebcast.com

---

CHAPTER 11

How High Sticker Price Colleges Can Cost Less Than "Cheaper" State Schools

I'm guessing you know that college is really, really expensive.[67] You may have seen stats that back this up (college costs have risen 1,000% in the past 30 years, compared to 700% for healthcare, 300% for inflation, yada yada yada).

But what do these percentages mean? As I write this in early 2018, one year at a state university can run around $25,000-55,000 (tuition, fees, room and board, etc.), depending on whether you're attending in-state or out-of-state.[68] A private college can cost more than $75,000 But **frequently, the net price of a seemingly more expensive college is less than a "cheaper" state college or university**.

How? Many private colleges and universities use their endowments to meet 85%, 90%, 95% or more of financial need. State colleges meet roughly 50-65%.

---

[67] I guess I am psychic! Look for my infomercial and 900 number hotline.
[68] Which I call, "The worst of both worlds" – higher rates as a non-resident, and state colleges have very little funding to give.

80

They also engage in a practice called "Leveraging," or "Preferential Packaging," meaning that they bribe students whom they want to come. This has nothing to do with your income or assets.

The umbrella term for this type of discounting is "Merit" aid. I find this term misleading, because when most parents hear the word merit or merit scholarship they think their child won't qualify if he doesn't have perfect SAT scores and a 5.0 average (out of 4.0). Then they start "SAT-Shaming" them until they hit 1500.

I think the better term is "Non Need-based," because there are plenty of B plus kids who receive $8,000, $12,000, $20,000 or more per year from private colleges.

I wrote this shortly after I ran into a client's kid, who was bussing tables at a new Italian place that opened up on the beach near our house. She had a C plus average and a heavy weed habit. But she got $22,000 per year from her top choice school! If she can get a big scholarship, why can't your kid?!

Colleges apply leveraging strategies to attract kids from affluent families, kids from parts of the country that are underrepresented at that college, etc. because they need to get tushies in seats![69] If

---

[69] Critics point out that this practice has resulted in less funding going to low income families. I'm just giving you the facts.

they charge 60K, but give a family earning 300K a discount of 12K, two things happen:

1. They still get 48K from the family; and

2. The kid gets to feel good that she earned a scholarship (and Mom gets to throw it in the face of her annoying sister-in-law who brags daily about her perfect daughter at Penn).

Since the mid-1990s, colleges have given more merit-based aid than need-based. The average discount rate at private colleges is 49.1%.[70] Average!

CNBC reported that 50% of students attending college receive a 90% discount.

Who gets this money? Not just low-income families – the majority goes to families from the top income quartile.

Which colleges do not give to six-figure-earning families? State universities. Not all, but most are not generous to "Forgotten Middle Class" families.

The Cost of Attendance at state universities - paying in-state tuition rates – runs around $25,000-30,000 at most schools. If you're an out-of-stater, it's close to $50,000 in many cases.

Colleges use "Net Price Calculators" to give information such as the following:

---

[70] According to the National Association of Collegiate Business Officers.

82

	State School	Private College
Cost Of Attendance	45,000	60,000
Discount	0	18,000
Net price	45,000	42,000

In this apples-to-apples comparison, the higher sticker priced private college costs a little less than the state school.

But that's not the end of the comparison, we'll talk "apples to oranges" in a moment.

First, consider that many students at large public school report:

- Their classes have 300-500 students enrolled;
- They're forced to watch an instructor on a television monitors or take classes online; and
- Their instructor is not a "real" professor, but rather a graduate assistant from a former Soviet Bloc country with a thick accent.

I am NOT bashing public colleges at all, many kids can handle them. Our oldest son attends one, as a matter of fact. But it's important to have your eyes wide open, and it's smart to discuss what your child's learning environment could look like. State universities are great for some kids, not so for others.

Now, let's examine an overlooked factor that impacts how much you'll pay for college.

CHAPTER 12

HOW LONG DOES IT REALLY TAKE TO GRADUATE?

The Six Year Plan

It's not so easy to get out of a public college in four years. Most college students take six years to get their degree according to the National Center For Education Statistics. SIX years!

Guess what the main culprit is? It's not because:

- Kids are goofing off and cutting class;
- They're running out of money;
- They're smoking happy grass or partying too much; or
- They're aimlessly switching majors and prolonging their college careers.

Sure, these issues contribute, but they're not the main problem.

The main reason students do not graduate in four years is because they can't get the classes they need to fulfill their majors

Classes at state schools tend to be oversubscribed, it's very hard to get a slot in a required course.

And it's not just because of overcrowding. Once they get tenure, professors have an easier time managing their massive teaching load (1-2 classes per semester) – and they can control their own schedules, in many cases. Example: they can teach Wednesdays at 11am every other year, even if it doesn't suit most students' schedules.

I'll put it another way. if you're a business major, you may not get Accounting 101 until your Junior year – and Accounting 102 for another two or three semesters. You're lower in priority than the 5th year, 4th year and other students who have been trying to get that class longer than you.

State universities are facing a perfect storm – budget cuts to prevent them hiring more staff and swelling enrollment. Their labor costs and costs of implementing state-of-the-art, cutting edge technology pose formidable budgetary constraints too. Every state in the union is crying the blues about being underfunded. I don't see this environment improving in the near term, if ever. Do you?

Check out these statistics reported by the Education Trust for a handful of public RWSCs Rear Window Sticker Colleges[71]):

---

[71] I made up this term, and am very proud of arguably my only original thought.

College	% Students Graduating in 4 Years
University of Michigan	75.6
University of Maryland	67.0
University of Delaware	68.0
Ohio State University	61.5
SUNY Binghamton	67.9
Penn State	65.6
UMASS Amherst	62.8
UNC Chapel HIll	80.4
University of Virginia	87.4
University Of South Carolina	55.6
University of Wisconsin	54.7

Although these numbers are dismal, there are some bright spots (UVA, UNC). And they have steadily improved since 2013 when I first published this book.

Your best bet is to plan on taking five years to graduate, but do whatever you can to stack the odds of a four-year sojourn in your favor (load up on AP classes, take a couple of summer classes, etc.) Now let's look at some private RWSCs, also in non-alphabetical or any other order:

College	% Students Graduation in 4 Years
American University	76.4
New York University	71.6
Boston College	88.1
Harvard	85.7
Penn	86.9
GWU	72.4
Providence College	83.2
Villanova	85.4
Syracuse	68.7
Boston University	79.5
University of Southern California	75.7
Elon	75.7
Duke	87.1
High Point	59.2
Williams	88.5

Here's the bottom line: with exception (e.g.High Point, George Washington University), you have a much better shot at completing your degree in four years at a private college, which typically has smaller classes and fewer over-enrollment issues.

CHAPTER 13

SOME COLLEGES ARE BETTER GIVERS THAN OTHERS

Although colleges use the same financial aid formulas, **they differ significantly in how much they award.** In other words, there are discrepancies about how they APPLY the financial aid formulas.

Generally speaking, older, prestigious colleges – Ivies and other private universities, offer significant amounts of aid, thanks to their large endowments (and perpetual fundraising, which starts before kids graduate!). Public universities offer very little financial aid as they rarely have endowment funding to spare. Instead, they award federal grants and loans.

All things being equal – like school reputation, how alums fare in the job market, "fit" and so forth – wouldn't you rather attend a school with more grants and scholarships?

I know the answer because you would not be reading this (nonrefundable) book otherwise. Here are some tips to help identify colleges that are likely to show you the lettuce:

Ask (research) these three questions:

1. What percentage of financial need does the college meet?

2. How is that need met (the percentage of free money - grants and scholarships - vs. loans and work study)?

3. What happens in years two, three, etc.? If your financial need stays the same, will your financial aid AWARD look substantially the same?

You can back into a lot of important information like these questions on the College Board website, and a little-known, cumbersome tool called The Common Data Set, a college-by-college breakdown of statistical information.

Resources: The Common Data Set, a format used by almost all colleges, CollegeBoard.org...and, oh yeah,our webinar, www.FinancialAidWebcast.com

Re: Common Data Set. If you want to research graduation rates, average award for all underclassmen, whatever for Notre Dame, Google "Common Data Set Notre Dame" for 31 pages of statistics (light reading!).

Final comment: Don't assume that similarly-ranked colleges are equally generous - sometimes there is no rhyme or reason to this whole mess!

CHAPTER 14

HOW "FORGOTTEN MIDDLE CLASS" FAMILIES RECEIVE JUICY GRANTS AND SCHOLARSHIPS

Since the mid-1990's. colleges and universities have publicly courted upper middle class families – regularly awarding five figure sums to parents with six figure incomes.

That's yet another reason you should not blow off filling out the financial aid paperwork, even if YOU think you won't qualify. One study showed that 53% of eligible families did not bother applying – leaving millions on the table.[72]

The University of Pennsylvania reports that families with income of $140,000 or more typically receive a 33% discount off tuition[73.]

US News & World Report says 46% of students at Fairfield University receive need-based aid, with the average grant award being $26,170.[74] (If you tour Fairfield you won't see too many

---

[72] I mentioned earlier that I saw this on the Internet. Now I'm repeating it here, in the same book. So it's double-true!

[73]   http://www.sfs.upenn.edu/paying/paying-pro-look-at-the-facts.htm

[74] https://www.usnews.com/best-colleges/fairfield-university-1385/paying

kids from low income families, but you will see a TON of Vineyard Vines clothing.)

The College Board reports that 88% of applicants for financial aid at Duke were approved for need-based aid with an average grant of $40,841[75]

So, let's say that you're considering Villanova and Wake Forest, two similarly-ranked schools. If you research their generosity on the College Board site, you'll see that Wake is much more generous (meeting 100% of need compared to 81% at Villanova) and therefore more likely to be cheaper to attend.

All of this information is publicly disclosed, you just have to roll up your sleeves and dig it up!

---

[75] https://bigfuture.collegeboard.org/college-university-search/duke-university

CHAPTER 15

COLLEGES WITH LOOSE PURSE STRINGS

Schools that meet 100% of Financial Need

Here's a list of the most generous colleges in America, according to *US News and World Report*. No way you've heard of all of 'em (yes, that's a challenge!):

Amherst College (MA)
Barnard College (NY)
Bates College (ME)
Boston College
Bowdoin College (ME)
Brown University (RI)
Bryn Mawr College (PA)
California Institute of Technology
Carleton College (MN)
Claremont McKenna College (CA)
Colby College (ME)
Colgate University (NY)
College of the Holy Cross (MA)
Colorado College

Columbia University (NY)
Connecticut College
Cornell University (NY)
Dartmouth College (NH)
Davidson College (NC)
Duke University (NC)
Franklin and Marshall College (PA)
Georgetown University (DC)
Grinnell College (IA)
Hamilton College (NY)
Harvard University (MA)
Harvey Mudd College (CA)
Haverford College (PA)
Johns Hopkins University (MD)
Kenyon College (OH)
Lafayette College (PA)
Macalester College (MN)
Massachusetts Institute of Technology
Middlebury College (VT)
Mount Holyoke College (MA)
Northwestern University (IL)
Oberlin College (OH)
Occidental College (CA)
Pitzer College (CA)
Pomona College (CA)
Princeton University (NJ)

Rice University (TX)
Salem College (NC)
Scripps College (CA)
Smith College (MA)
Stanford University (CA)
Swarthmore College (PA)
Thomas Aquinas College (CA)
Trinity College (CT)
Tufts University (MA)
Union College (NY)
University of Chicago
University of North Carolina—Chapel Hill
University of Notre Dame (IN)
University of Pennsylvania
University of Richmond (VA)
University of Southern California
University of Virginia
Vanderbilt University (TN)
Vassar College (NY)
Wake Forest University (NC)
Washington and Lee University (VA)
Washington University in St. Louis
Wellesley College (MA)
Wesleyan University (CT)
Williams College (MA)

Yale University (CT)

CHAPTER 16

LARGEST COLLEGE ENDOWMENTS 2019

Here's a fun chart (aren't they all fun?) from the Dep't of Ed: colleges with the largest endowments. The data is for fiscal year 2016, published in 2019.

Endowment funds of the 20 colleges and universities with the largest endowments, by rank order: Fiscal year (FY) 2016			
		Market value of endowment (in thousands of dollars)	
Institution	Rank order[1]	Beginning of FY	End of FY
United States, all institutions		$553,509,685	$542,240,202
Harvard University (MA)	1	37,615,545	35,665,743
Yale University (CT)	2	25,542,983	25,413,149
University of Texas System Office	3	22,548,856	23,861,771
Stanford University (CA)	4	22,222,957	22,398,130
Princeton University (NJ)	5	22,291,270	21,703,488
Massachusetts Institute of Technology	6	13,474,743	13,181,515
University of Pennsylvania	7	10,133,569	10,715,364
Texas A & M University, College Station	8	9,754,202	9,858,672
University of Michigan, Ann Arbor	9	9,809,705	9,600,640
Columbia University in the City of New York (NY)	10	9,639,065	9,041,027
University of Notre Dame (IN)	11	8,784,381	8,748,266
University of California System Admin. Central Office	12	6,950,190	8,367,764
Northwestern University (IL)	13	7,588,029	7,478,167
Emory University (GA)	14	6,787,163	6,902,625
Duke University (NC)	15	7,296,545	6,839,760
Washington University in St. Louis (MO)	16	6,889,230	6,526,726
University of Chicago (IL)	17	6,553,571	6,121,266
University of Virginia, Main Campus	18	6,098,997	5,774,744
Rice University (TX)	19	5,573,038	5,354,508
University of Southern California	20	4,709,511	4,608,714

CHAPTER 17

THE HIDDEN TRUTH ABOUT SCHOLARSHIPS

Scholarships are fun to talk about[76] over coffee, the water cooler or Facebook, but the chit chat isn't all true, alas. Much is, dare I say, "Fake News."

This book is focused more on going after the big money, from college endowments, but I'd be remiss if I didn't spend some time on other, "outside" scholarships that do not come from colleges.

First, you should never have to pay a service that finds scholarships for you. Stay far away from any company that guarantees or pressures you to sign up. I have yet to come across a paid service that does something that you cannot do quickly and easily yourself – at no cost.

On the other hand, it can be worth working with a scholarship coach, who helps with the search, the applications and essays. We are not in that line of business, so I recommend Ashley Hill,[77] who has worked with our clients for more than two years now.

---

[76]i.e., "brag about"

[77] www.CollegePrepReady.com

There are plenty of free scholarship search sites online. Here are a few – I cannot vouch personally for any but these sites were active when I wrote this. I put in a solid nine minutes making certain they still worked, you are the beneficiary of the fruits of my labor!

www.FastWeb.com

www.MyScholly.com

www.CollegeBoard.org

www.MeritAid.com

www.CollegeAnswer.com

www.Scholarships.com

www.CollegeNet.com

www.College-Scholarships.com

www.FastAid.com

I deal with scams in the next chapter.

A word on itty-bitty little scholarships. A $500 scholarship may seem like small potatoes, but plenty of them are renewable. So a $500 scholarship really represents $2,000, in most cases. Get a bunch of them and they start to add up.

The other thing about little scholarships is that they tend to be less competitive, because fewer kids do the work to uncover them because of the leg work involved (not YOUR kids, of course).

The above-mentioned websites, on the other hand, are pretty highly visible online and attract a lot of traffic, making your competition tougher.

There are tons of local scholarships worth checking out. The best place to start your research is your high school guidance counselor. He or she should have a list of local organizations and scholarships, such as:

The Rotary Club

The Chamber of Commerce

The Elks

The VFW

Kiwanis

The Jaycees

Booster Clubs

Etc. etc. etc.

Here's a sneaky "Ninja" tactic: look up *other high schools'* **guidance counselor lists.** Nice, right?

Another place to look for local scholarships is in the local paper(s). They report scholarship winners all the time. Research the entity or institution that awarded the scholarship, contact them and inquire about their scholarship qualification process. (The more work involved, the less likely your fellow competitor-peers will do the same thing.)

Also, keep in mind that there are plenty of scholarships reserved for "regular" students –kids who are not valedictorians, did not achieve perfect SAT scores and did not broker a meaningful, long-lasting peace in the Middle East during last summer's life changing 10-day trip.

Scholarships and Need-based Aid

Now let me warn you about scholarships' relationship with need-based financial aid.[78] It is entirely possible, that after dozens of man-hours spent researching scholarship requirements, drafting and redrafting of essays and other agony, your child will have cobbled $2,500 worth of scholarships from six sources.

Now, fast-forward to March of the senior year of high school, as the financial aid award letters start rolling in. Each school offering you money will also ask if you received any "outside" scholarships or financial assistance.

---

[78] Now that I think about it, maybe this part should have been at the beginning of the chapter. Ooops.

You'll tell them "Yes, 2,500 clams from the Knights of The Holy Grail Virtual Quidditch Club."

Guess what happens now? The college financial aid office will reduce their award by $2,500, because your financial aid award was based on your RESOURCES. And your hard work created more resources! A "nice" financial aid office will reduce the loan portion of the award first, but you should be aware of this possible outcome.

If you're not going to qualify for need-based financial aid, ignore what I just told you, the award reduction scenario doesn't apply to merit scholarships offered by the college.

But there is big money in the federal need-based system (more than $240 Billion). If you are going to request and qualify for need-based financial aid, please be careful about the amount of time you spend chasing this loose change!

CHAPTER 18

AVOID SCHOLARSHIP SEARCH SCAMS

Here are a few guidelines on sniffing out a scholarship scam. Avoid solicitations such as:

We'll guarantee you a scholarship or your money back!

Congratulations, you're a finalist! (Even though you didn't enter a contest.)

You cannot get this information anywhere else!

This scholarship costs some money.

We need your credit card number to "reserve" or "hold" your scholarship.

Obama/Trump/Oprah Wants Single Moms to Go Back to School! (A marketing gimmick for adult education providers who pay for leads generated by these types of ads)

The bottom line is that you should avoid any high-pressure tactics or sales-pitchy language – even if you just can't seem to put your finger on why you're getting the heebie-jeebies.

If you do get scammed you should report it to some or all of the below:

Local police precinct – Economic Crimes

The post office (if you received direct mail and signed up with a scammy service): usps.com

Your District Attorney's Office

The Federal Trade Commission FTC.gov/scholarshipscams

The National Consumers League Fraud Information Center – www.fraud.org

I can't speak to how fast any of these organizations will move if you report something to them, but I can say unequivocally that these organizations take scholarship scams very seriously.

CHAPTER 19

THOSE COLLEGE BOARD SNEAKY SONS OF BITCHES

Pardon my salty language, but I was watching Frost – Nixon back when I originally wrote this, and that phrase featured prominently in Richard Nixon's repertoire.

I've mentioned the College Board repeatedly throughout this book because they do a great job at giving important information about colleges.

They also administer the SAT, which you probably know. But let me 'learn ya a few other interesting facts about this "Nonprofit Institution of Higher Education."

The College Board was a student lender until October 2007, when it was accused of…wait for it… "Deceptive marketing practices" by two then-attorneys general, Cuomo (NY) and Blumenthal (CT). They settled this lawsuit, paid a stiff fine and stopped lending.[79]

---

[79]

http://www.bloomberg.com/apps/news?pid=newsarchive&sid=acYV wF0t1ykE&refer=us

According to Blumenthal, "The College Board provided discounted equipment and services to the schools in exchange for a coveted spot on the schools' preferred-lender lists" without disclosing this arrangement to parents.

Cuomo called this arrangement "deceitful."

I'd call it a "kickback."

But that's old news. The College Board is in another line of business that you may know about, hiding in plain sight:

Selling data. YOUR data.

If your child has registered for the SAT, you're experiencing it first-hand: a trickle, then a flood of direct mail from a ton of schools you never heard of.

How do these colleges find you? You guessed it, through the College Board.

For a very reasonable set up fee of $15,000 plus a not-so-reasonable 70 cents per record, colleges can search the College Board's records by:

Grades

Scores

Ethnicity

Sex

Zip Code

Other "Selects"

How big is this business? Big. Northeastern University sends 200,000 pieces of direct mail each year to get 60,000 applications. At 70 cents per head (not including the setup fee), that's a cool $140,000 the College Board made off one college alone.

There are close to 2,600 four-year colleges in the country. If 20% of them spend half as much as Northeastern, that's a deep seven figure source of income for the good old College Board.

No matter how you slice it, the College Board makes millions outside of its "core" test prep business. $840 Mill in fiscal 2014.

Not bad for a non-profit!

Form **990**	**Return of Organization Exempt From Income Tax**	OMB No. 1545-0047
	Under section 501(c), 527, or 4947(a)(1) of the Internal Revenue Code (except private foundations)	**2013**
Department of the Treasury / Internal Revenue Service	▶ Do not enter Social Security numbers on this form as it may be made public. ▶ Information about Form 990 and its instructions is at www.irs.gov/form990.	Open to Public Inspection

A For the 2013 calendar year, or tax year beginning JULY 01, 2013, and ending JUNE 30, 20 14

B Check if applicable:
- ☐ Address change
- ☐ Name change
- ☐ Initial return
- ☐ Terminated
- ☐ Amended return
- ☐ Application pending

C Name of organization COLLEGE ENTRANCE EXAMINATION BOARD
Doing Business As THE COLLEGE BOARD
Number and street (or P.O. box if mail is not delivered to street address) 250 VESEY STREET   Room/suite
City or town, state or province, country, and ZIP or foreign postal code NEW YORK, NY 10281

D Employer identification number 13-1623965
E Telephone number (212)713-8000
G Gross receipts $ 908,653,248

F Name and address of principal officer: DAVID COLEMAN
SAME AS C ABOVE

H(a) Is this a group return for subordinates? ☐ Yes ☑ No
H(b) Are all subordinates included? ☐ Yes ☐ No
If "No," attach a list. (see instructions)

I Tax-exempt status: ☑ 501(c)(3) ☐ 501(c)( ) ◀ (insert no.) ☐ 4947(a)(1) or ☐ 527
J Website: ▶ WWW.COLLEGEBOARD.ORG
K Form of organization: ☑ Corporation ☐ Trust ☐ Association ☐ Other ▶
L Year of formation: 1900
H(c) Group exemption number ▶
M State of legal domicile: NY

Part I **Summary**

1 Briefly describe the organization's mission or most significant activities: FOUNDED IN 1900, THE COLLEGE BOARD WAS CREATED TO EXPAND ACCESS TO HIGHER EDUCATION. WE ARE A MISSION-DRIVEN, MEMBERSHIP ORGANIZATION MADE UP OF OVER 6,000 OF THE WORLD'S LEADING COLLEGES. (CONTINUED ON SCHEDULE O)

2 Check this box ▶ ☐ if the organization discontinued its operations or disposed of more than 25% of its net assets.

3	Number of voting members of the governing body (Part VI, line 1a)	3	31
4	Number of independent voting members of the governing body (Part VI, line 1b)	4	30
5	Total number of individuals employed in calendar year 2013 (Part V, line 2a)	5	1,856
6	Total number of volunteers (estimate if necessary)	6	473
7a	Total unrelated business revenue from Part VIII, column (C), line 12	7a	-461,005
b	Net unrelated business taxable income from Form 990-T, line 34	7b	

		Prior Year	Current Year
8	Contributions and grants (Part VIII, line 1h)	7,569,739	8,058,498
9	Program service revenue (Part VIII, line 2g)	771,895,617	813,419,085
10	Investment income (Part VIII, column (A), lines 3, 4, and 7d)	16,352,246	19,195,407
11	Other revenue (Part VIII, column (A), lines 5, 6d, 8c, 9c, 10c, and 11e)	0	0
12	Total revenue—add lines 8 through 11 (must equal Part VIII, column (A), line 12)	795,817,602	840,672,990
13	Grants and similar amounts paid (Part IX, column (A), lines 1–3)	5,046,333	909,647
14	Benefits paid to or for members (Part IX, column (A), line 4)	0	0
15	Salaries, other compensation, employee benefits (Part IX, column (A), lines 5–10)	210,846,888	199,254,431
16a	Professional fundraising fees (Part IX, column (A), line 11e)	0	0
b	Total fundraising expenses (Part IX, column (D), line 25) ▶ 317,616		
17	Other expenses (Part IX, column (A), lines 11a–11d, 11f–24e)	524,666,464	541,614,047
18	Total expenses. Add lines 13–17 (must equal Part IX, column (A), line 25)	740,561,685	741,778,125
19	Revenue less expenses. Subtract line 18 from line 12	55,255,917	98,894,865
		Beginning of Current Year	End of Year

Incidentally, the reason the SAT changed format recently is because the College Board lost market share to its arch-rival, the ACT.

Or maybe that's a coincidence?[80]

---

[80] Feel the snark dripping off this page.

CHAPTER 20

MERIT MONEY FOR THE AFFLUENT

Let's assume that you can't qualify for need-based financial aid. Are you screwed?

YES! Loser.

KIdding! It's far from Game Over.

Countless private – and many state – colleges will regularly bribe, um, "incentivize" students of affluent families to attend their schools.

Why would a college do this? Here are the main reasons.

1. To raise their rankings. A student with high grades and standardized scores will boost a college's *US News and World Report* rank, so it could be worth a $15,000 tuition discount to help climb the rankings ladder. Tulane University is one of many colleges notorious for this.

2. To curry favor (called "Development"). Example: Once Parker Whitebread Pewterschmidt III[81] enrolls, the college cold-

---

[81] "Looking good, Parker!" "Feeling good, Todd."

callers will descend on him and Daddy like a Jersey Shore cast-member hitting the tanning salon:

Early, often and unctuously. They are betting that Parker will be inclined to become a loyal financial supporter for years as he recalls his glory days over a few brewskies at Alumni Weekend, before vomiting.

3. To compete with the Ivies and other "Tier One" colleges. Example: Ivies, "Little Ivies" like Amherst and Williams and other DIII schools and other conferences don't award athletic scholarships *per se*, but I see these guidelines getting bent every year. Need is in the eye of the beholder, I guess.

4. The overriding, most important reason: to get butts in seats! Kids and parents hardly ever think about this, because they're so busy chasing colleges around, but colleges want them just as badly. Particularly kids from upper middle class neighborhoods whose families can pay in full, but would love the bragging rights of a $15,000 merit award. For an eye-opening article, see this piece in the *New York Times* Education Section:

https://www.nytimes.com/interactive/2019/09/10/magazine/college-admissions-paul-tough.html

When I first wrote this book, I personally witnessed two C plus/B minus clients receive awards between $15,000-22,000 per year from their top choice schools. I've seen this happen repeatedly.

If a kid has at least a B + average, there are scores of suitable colleges that would happily award similar amounts, even larger.

> The College Board - CollegeBoard.org and the Common Data set (discussed previously) is a great source of information in this area. Look up each college's reported 'Non-Need Based Aid" average award statistics.

Pet Strategy

One of my favorite recommendations is to have clients apply to one or two colleges solely because they compete with other schools on the applicant's list. In other words, schools that have historically vied for the same type of student.

Then, after we get a scholarship offers from the strategically chosen colleges, we play the schools off against each other, attempting to improve them.

Does this sound cold, ruthless and mercenary?

That's because it is. It's strictly business.[82]

I cover this technique more in a separate chapter on negotiations. And I teach a class on it, which includes sample letters of appeals

---

[82] Don Andy Lockwoodeone

and other bonus materials to help you make the college a counter offer they can't refuse.

Let's see if I have the website handy...oh, yeah, here! www.AppealsClass.com.

CHAPTER 21

DO GRADES HAVE ANYTHING TO DO WITH FINANCIAL AID AWARDS?

I wanted to address one of the biggest misconceptions about need-based financial aid – the apparent link between academic achievement and financial aid awards.

Many parents assume that their child must have outstanding grades to qualify for grants and scholarships. Not true.

Except when they do.

Here's the deal. Need-based awards are based on your Expected Family Contribution, which is used to calculate your financial need. EFC includes more than 70 factors, none of which is related to academic stuff. (It's income, assets, age of parent, number of kids in college and more. Covered above and on our financial aid webinar that I have mentioned 46 times by now.[83])

Broadly speaking – if you're bright enough to get in, you're in. If you need money, you get money.

---

[83] Fine. www.FinancialAidWebcast.com.

Of course, there are exceptions to this rule. And I will freely confess that, all things being equal on paper between two families – income, assets, etc. – the child with superior academic achievement, or the recruited athlete, or kid who is an underrepresented minority, will likely do better across the board than a competitor child from the other family.

Not politically-correct but true. Even from the so-called "need-blind" colleges.

How do I reconcile this?

I already have. Financial aid officers, particularly those at elite, competitive colleges with their own institutional money, can use Professional Discretion to sweeten the offer for those whom they deem to be desirable applicants.

Earlier, I mentioned student athletes. Ivy League schools do not award athletic scholarships (contrary to what you heard from the Dad at the gym whose kid got a "full ride" for lacrosse to Princeton[84]). But athletes frequently receive more of a "grant-in-need" than their non-athletic counterparts who look nearly identical on paper, income and asset-wise. "Need is in the eye of the beholder," to quote a really, really smart college advisor.

Wait! This isn't fair!

---

[84] Said 1. to brag and 2. to justify 10 years and six figures worth of money sunk into travel teams and private coaching sessions.

Your point?

Don't get hung up on "fair," because this process is not designed to be fair.

We're talking about the college's endowment, meaning it's their money and they can do what they want with it. Frequently, endowment gifts come with certain stipulations. It's common for donors to stipulate heir bequests earmarked for athletes, musicians, kids who are going to study environmental science, women's studies or whatever cause they want to advance.

That's just the way it is, my friend! Even if you think it's unfair.

CHAPTER 22

TO ASK OR NOT TO ASK

If you check the "Yes – I want Financial Aid" box, will it hurt your chances of admission?

Lori, a slender, dark haired 40-something mom sat across from me, with a conflicted, pained expression.

"Should we apply for financial aid? Or will it hurt Carly's chances of getting in?"

Carly's first choice college was Duke. She was a great student at one of the top high schools near my office, and had terrific extra-curricular activities.

But there was a whole other – emotional – part of her story.

Three years ago, Carly's dad, Jeff, an outgoing, hard-charging, entrepreneurial guy, died in a freak accident.

Lori felt that her husband would have wanted Carly to go to the best school she could, no matter what the price, as a reward for her hard work. After all, he left Lori with a sizeable life insurance payout (although, after Lori paid off the mortgage and took a look at college costs for her two kids, it didn't feel quite as big).

Here's the first part of what I told her.

Need Blind

Duke is "need-blind" – meaning they make admissions decisions without regard to whether the applicant needs financial aid. That's the party line at Duke and every need-blind school, at least.

Is this really true? First, no admissions or financial aid officer at any need-blind college will admit, on the record, that they consider whether a child wants financial aid. For the most part, even I, Cynical Andy, believe them.

They say that, if your child is good enough to get into a college, whether he or she needs financial aid is a separate issue. That's why financial aid offices and admissions offices are frequently located in separate wings, even separate buildings – to keep things apart.

Most need-blind colleges are highly competitive – they admit less than 20% - sometimes less than 10%, even 6% - of their applicants. They reject thousands of applicants for every one they admit.

Need Aware

The other category is "Need Aware" colleges – those that consider whether the applicant wants financial aid as ONE of the 20-25 factors evaluated (grades, strength of course load, standardized test scores, recommendations, etc.) They lump kids into two categories.

When an application comes in, it gets placed in one of two piles – those who requested aid ("Needs Aid") or those who didn't request aid ("Full Pricers"). Each pile is huge.

A college knows ahead of time that 75% of its freshman class will receive aid and 25% will not.[85] If the admissions officer rejects one candidate from the "Needs Aid" pile, there are still thousands of wannabes to take up the slack.

Same with the Full Pricers.

That's the textbook explanation of the two types of colleges. Let's look at reality.

Here's what I REALLY told Lori. The gist was that, embarrassingly, I was superstitious enough to NOT check the box, because there just might be a remote possibility that doing so could *slightly* decrease Carly's chances of admission.

"OK," she said. "What if somehow Carly manages to get in, and then we go back and fill out the financial aid forms?"

I gave one of my famous boilerplate answers.

"I can almost promise you that you will lose out – probably not entirely, but you will receive 10%, 20% or some amount less than if you had applied for financial aid at the outset."

---

[85] Approximately!

Why? Because admissions officers and financial aid officers know EXACTLY what you're doing. They've seen it all.

I explained that she'd get less because they don't like the way she's played the game.

So Carly applied Early Decision. She did not request aid, because she and Lori thought her dad would not have wanted her to.

A month later, Duke deferred her to the main, regular decision pool, which Lori and I joked was a major accomplishment, since Carly was a "Plain White Girl" from Long Island.[86]

Carly submitted applications to several other schools. As she started to get acceptances, we quickly submitted the financial aid applications.

Then, one day in early March, Lori called me.

"Carly got into Duke!"

"Whoa – that's awesome!" I said. "Let's get the financial aid forms in ASAP!"

"What should we say about why we didn't apply before?" She asked. "And can they cancel her acceptance?"

---

[86] Competitive schools like Duke reserve up to 80% (not a misprint) of their slots for non-academic reasons: recruited athletes, legacies, minorities, international students and other "hooks." See *Admissions Confidential* by Rachel Toor.

I suggested that we tell them that their guidance counselor said that she wouldn't qualify (which was true), so she didn't bother applying, And I reassured Lori that Duke would not rescind their offer.

We rushed in the financial aid applications. A week later, we heard back:

Loans only. $5,500. Crap.

"Is this because we delayed filing?" Lori asked (the original deadline was November 1st, it was now the middle of March).

"I'm sure that has something to do with it, but we should appeal. It's not like Duke ran out of money in the last couple of months," I said.

So we put together a letter, outlining information that Duke didn't know, including that Lori had just returned to the workforce part-time, and her assets were really life insurance proceeds that constituted the bulk of her savings – she had little in the way of IRAs or other retirement savings, and had eight years of college expenses ahead between the two children.

The financial aid officer assigned to Lori was responsive and really nice, writing a long, heartfelt reply along the lines of "Let me see what I can do."

Two weeks later, the revised offer arrived: $17,000 in grants!

Lori was thrilled! I was ecstatic, and imagined that Jeff was looking down, also pleased.

CHAPTER 23

AN EARLY DECISION FACT YOU'LL NEVER HEAR FROM YOUR GUIDANCE COUNSELOR

Why do kids apply Early Decision? First, a note on the difference between ED (yet another acronym) and Early Action. If you apply ED and if accepted, you must attend.[87]

Well, sorta. There is a rarely-discussed "financial out" if you decide that the award is inadequate.

Note: This is one of those things that surprises the starch out of most parents I speak to. My theory is that their guidance counselors are gun-shy about telling them this, out of fear that, if this right is invoked, the affected college will "black ball" the high school the following year. (No, I can't prove this.)

Early Action (EA), on the other hand is non-binding.

ED boosts chances of admission at most colleges, not all. EA barely helps, if at all.

---

[87] Even though people younger than 18 are minors who lack the legal capacity to enter into a contract, don't get me started. ED is just that – an offer (from the kid –"If you admit me, I'm coming!") and an acceptance ("OK!" from the college.)

On the other hand, stronger students tend to apply ED as do recruited athletes and applicants recommended by trustees and other "connected" folks. In other words, ED stats are skewed because of this self-selection.

ED helps, but not as much as the statistics might lead you to believe.

Actually, it helps a TON. Helps admissions officers fill their class, that is.

Next, let's look at the potential - and very real - negative effect applying ED could have on your financial aid package!

CHAPTER 24

WILL APPLYING EARLY HURT YOUR CHANCES OF FINANCIAL AID?

Even the Early Bird gets screwed sometimes

You know that applying Early Decision and Early Action dramatically help your chances of admission. But what's the effect on financial aid awards?

My feeling, admittedly based on anecdotal evidence[88]– is that you'd better be careful about applying Early Decision if you need financial aid.

Why? Sometimes colleges will intentionally under-award an applicant who deserves more on paper. Guess why this happens?

Because colleges would rather that you pay more instead of less! Genius![89]

---

[88] As opposed to the rigorous scientific data elsewhere in this treatise.
[89] Did you post your 5 star rating for this book yet?

So it's as if the financial aid officer is sitting there with your file, thinking "Hmmm, Brandon deserves $27,000...but let's see if he'll come for $18,500? Bwah hahahahaha!!!"

That's a slight exaggeration of what goes on...I think. But the concept is important:

If you are contractually bound to attend a college, you lose a big bargaining chip in terms of financial aid.

My client Claire ignored my advice[90] and applied ED to Emory.

On December 15th, she received great good news – she got in!

The bad news came two days later – her parents got shafted in financial aid – a bunch of loans, no free money.

"What happened," her dad Scott asked. "Was it because we applied Early Decision?"

"I'm sure that had something to do with it, but this is awful," I said.

"I think it's one of two things," I said. "Either they made some kind of mistake, which I doubt, or they think you make more money than you show on paper," I said.

---

[90] Always gratifying.

Ironically, a few weeks later, the *New York Times* wrote a story about exactly this practice, featuring Emory.[91] It's almost like I made it into the *Times!*

Scott is a self-employed professional, who lives in an affluent area but does not show much income on his tax returns.

Turns out that we were faced with a strange task – showing somehow that Scott DIDN'T make more money. In other words, proving a negative - the absence of income.

When Scott called Emory's financial aid office, they asked him a few questions, one of which was about his mortgage payments. It was clear that they could not see how Scott could afford to live where he lived, on the income that he disclosed.

Scott informed the financial aid officer that he had recently refinanced their mortgage to lower their payments.

Emory told Scott to send a new mortgage payment stub to show the new amount.

But there was a little hitch – Claire had to either accept Emory's offer or withdraw her application by January 15th. Scott asked if they could reassess his daughter's award by then. Emory's response:

"We'll get back to you in April." (!)

---

[91] http://www.nytimes.com/2012/12/23/education/poor-students-struggle-as-class-plays-a-greater-role-in-success.html?pagewanted=all&_r=1&

Scott was understandably stressed out, "How can we possibly make a decision to attend if we don't know what our award will be for three months?" he asked.

I didn't have a good answer. In the formulas, he deserved at least $20,000. All I could say was that I seriously doubted that they'd give that amount, exuding my standard unbridled optimism.

"They could give you nothing, they could give you 10 grand. You either have to roll the dice and wait until April, or withdraw your application. I don't see any other options."

They decided to gamble and accept. I thought they were crazy, but kept that to myself.

What happened next was the crazy thing!

First, the aforementioned *New York Times* article about "lowball" offers came out, Scott and I emailed it to each other simultaneously.

"Is this what you were talking about?" Scott wrote.

"Yes!" I replied.

We waited. And waited. Nothing happened in February or March.

Then, days before Emory's April 1st deadline, they sent a revised offer: $38,000! (Actually, $38,579. Round numbers don't exist in financial aid.)

No explanation, just "here's the new offer."

We dodged a bullet! Scott and his family were ecstatic, I was dumbfounded.

How much did that article in the *Times* help? We'll never know.

Although it worked out for Scott and Emma, please understand that this is the exception, not the rule.

Be very, very careful about applying ED!

CHAPTER 25

"BLACK HAT" NEGOTIATING TACTICS

How to improve a crappy financial aid offer…even if you don't have compromising photos of the Dean

Before we get to the nuts and bolts of this chapter, did you know that your financial aid award is an offer? Many parents do not understand this – they assume that the award letter is final – a "take it or leave it" proposition.

It's not.

You can *appeal* a financial aid award. And if you're comparing offers from competing, similar schools – like George Washington and Syracuse, for example – NOT Princeton vs. Big Lou's Air Conditioning Lyceum[92] – you can play them off against one another, sometimes even when a college says "We don't do that here." Here are my suggestions on how to mount a successful appeal after a college "low-balls" you.

1. Your tone should be courteous, grateful and respectful – not pissy, angry or entitled. (I had a client who told his son's first

---

[92] They recruited me for basketball. Go Chillers!

choice school, "Please tell me how you can justify charging $15,000 more per year than Tulane..." That appeal did not go far.) You get more flies with honey than vinegar[93]. Start the letter by thanking the financial aid office for its generous offer.

2. CC the admissions officer assigned to your file. Most admissions offices divide up the country by region, assigning officers to areas of the country.

3. Understand that the admissions department cares very much about "Yield" – the number of applicants compared to the number of students who actually matriculate on campus. The higher the yield, the better the college looks in *US News and World Report*, among its college peers and other stakeholders like bondholders and trustees.

4. Explain that, while the offer on the table is generous, the other, competitor college's offer is better.

5. Explain that your child would MUCH prefer to attend your fine institution, but without additional aid, this dream will, alas, go unfulfilled.

6. If your child is *objectively* exceptional in any meaningful way – this is your opportunity to highlight that and "resell" the college on why your student will add to the college community.

---

[93] Assuming you actually want flies. (I never really understood this expression...)

Admissions officers at competitive colleges try to "build classes," meaning they look closely at what each child potentially brings to the table and what he'll bring to the college community. They'll look for athletes, drama students, journalists, musicians, politically active students and so forth.

On this topic, I recommend *The Gatekeepers* by Jacques Steinberg, former Education Writer for the New York Times. It's a behind-the-scenes look at the admissions process at Wesleyan University.[94]

> RESOURCE/SHAMELESS PLUG: I teach a "Master Class," with materials such as sample appeal letters that worked, that will walk you through each and every argument you can make the financial aid office after a stingy offer. And I will even review your appeal before you send it! See www.AppealsClass.com

7. Another tip – without going overboard, do not hesitate to tell the financial aid office about certain hardships that may not have been disclosed within the "four corners" of the financial aid application you submitted. This is your chance to let it all hang out – do not let your pride or shame get in the way – be emotional and be very, very descriptive if you are comfortable doing so.

Check that – do this even if you're not so comfortable! The stakes are too high to let your ego get in the way.

---

[94] Full disclosure - my alma mater. Not sure why I felt the need to inform you.

8. My final word of advice on this topic is do NOT, ahem, "bluff!" Don't get cute and imply that you received a better award elsewhere unless it's completely true. Because the financial aid office you're writing to could want to verify that you're not BS'ing them.

CHAPTER 26

DIVORCED AND SEPARATED FAMILIES

When "Mr. Wrong" can turn into "Mr. Right"

Many parents from divorced families make a mistake on the financial aid forms. They assume that, if they declare the child as a dependent for tax purposes, that means that they are the "custodial" parent for FAFSA purposes, and must file the FAFSA for their child.

But it ain't necessarily so. **FAFSA cares about the parent with whom the child spends the majority of his/her time – anything over 50%.**

In many divorces, the parents alternate who declares the child as a dependent, each year, thus claiming the deduction and lowering their tax bills.

But the IRS regulations are *different than* the Department of Education. The financial aid rules allow for a child to live with a parent who does not declare that child as a dependent. Kapeesh?

I have a client, Gary, who's self-employed – he runs a couple of dance studios. He shows hardly any money (profits) on paper, in fact, he filed bankruptcy a few years ago.

Gary's college-aged two kids split their time between him and his ex-wife. His ex is a physical therapist, who earns a nice salary. She filed the FAFSA for each of their two children.

Big mistake – the family would have tripled their eligibility if Gary were the "nominee" on the FAFSA – he shows hardly any income and, equally important, could say in good faith that his kids resided with him a majority of time.

What if your child spends more time with the high-earning, divorced parents? Maybe you rethink these living arrangements for financial aid purposes.

Don't do anything unethical,[95] but remember, the standard you must meet is that the child must spend "most" of his/her time with the custodial parent. Most means 50.000000001% in the 12 months leading up to the financial aid application submission date.

Story No. 2: I had a client, Marc, a couple of years ago who, according to his financial aid forms, resided with his self-employed father on the South Shore of Long Island. Yet,

---

[95] I'm not judging, just covering my butt in case you do something stupid, get caught and then say, "I read about it in this guy's book!"

somehow he attended high school 20 miles away on the North Shore, where his mother lived, coincidentally!

Even though that last paragraph dripped with sarcasm, it's factually accurate, thank you very much.

Marc cleaned up financial aid-wise at George Washington, which, at the time, cared only about the custodial parent. And the following year, he did really well, academically. So well that he applied to transfer to Georgetown, and got in!

But there was an issue. Georgetown looks at the financials of both the custodial and non-custodial parent. Marc's award from Georgetown was much worse than GW's, which looked at one parent's info only, at the time. He stayed at GW.

You probably noticed I said "at the time." GW used to care only about the custodial parent, not any more. Now GW requires the non-custodial parent to complete his own CSS Profile.. Things change so fast in the wonderful world of financial aid!!!

If a college requires the CSS Profile, there is a good chance - not a certainty - it will require the non-custodial parent to file a CSS Profile too. Check with each college on your list if it requires it.

Because I am a prince among men, here is where you can find a list of colleges requiring the CSS Profile, accurate as of the time of writing. You're welcome!

https://profile.collegeboard.org/profile/ppi/participatingInstitutions.aspx

IDOC

AFter you dutifully clicked that link, you might have noticed a column titled "IDOC." IDOC is a system used to transmit your tax info to each college subscribing to it. It's the equivalent of the IRS Data Retrieval Tool, which connects with the FAFSA to do substantially the same thing: port over your tax information.

Wondering why you might need to do both IDOC and IRS DRT?

Why does the sun rise or a wave wave? Who cares. They just do.[96]

What if a divorced parent remarries?

FAFSA counts "Household Income," meaning the new husband or wife's finances ARE part of the equation. Even if New Hubby has no legal or ethical obligation to support the college-bound kid from the divorced family. It's not about their obligation, it's about their *resources.*

Financial aid officers may exercise, Professional Judgment to consider any and all non-formulaic factors, so they will adjust an Expected Family Contribution on occasion, including situations like this. Sometimes.

---

[96] Did your review drop to 4 stars?

Another common question divorced parents ask (always moms): "What if my ex won't contribute a nickel toward college? Do I still need to force him to fill out the Non-Custodial Profile?"

Ah, the Deadbeat Dad.[97] You should inform the financial aid office if this is your reality. Many schools recognize that ex-spouses can be extremely uncooperative and will consider that when awarding financial aid. They will have you sign a waiver.

But not all will believe you. Some (like BU, in my experience) will take the approach that it's not their problem that Deadbeat Dad won't cooperate. They'll either refuse to consider the financial aid application at all, or they'll assign an arbitrary Expected Family Contribution to DD.

The bottom line is that all may not be lost if your ex is not cooperating, the financial aid office will usually accommodate you.

---

[97] Never a Deadbeat Mom...

CHAPTER 27

HOW IS MONEY AWARDED?

What does a financial aid package look like – loans, scholarships, what?

OK, time for a review question!

What is "financial aid?" Is it all loans?

Financial aid is an umbrella term. It means free money – grants and scholarships – and "self-help" – loans and work study.

Different colleges dole out awards in different ways. The more elite colleges with larger endowments tend to award 80% and up in free funding, while the land-grant, public universities might award packages 50% grants/scholarships, 50% loans/work study.

Let's look at this stuff one-by-one.

Although the term financial aid means only three things: loans, work-study and "free stuff" (grants, scholarships), the total amount of aid, and HOW it's awarded, varies greatly by college.

A perplexing issue is that, especially when it comes to loans, colleges use different terms (pun intended)[98] .

So a Stafford Subsidized Loan is now called the Direct Subsidized Loan.

Ditto for the Stafford Unsubsidized Loan and the Direct Unsubsidized Loan.

Some colleges "award" you a Parent Loan (PLUS), but this product is no award - it's a loan. The PLUS loan is a federally mandated "gap filler" designed to help you pay the difference between:

1. The total Cost of Attendance at the college, and

2. The amount of financial aid received.

Colleges now require loan counseling before they allow the student to accept funds, in a (halfass) effort to cut down on excessive borrowing, I suppose.

Much of the communication from a financial aid office or lender goes to the student, not the parent. Make sure your child knows this and checks his email regularly. (As I was writing another part of this book, I got an email from a kid, panicking, because he hadn't received his loan paperwork from the school. Turns out that it was sitting in his inbox from five weeks ago.)

---

[98] Loans have terms - the length of time you have to repay, interest, fees...never mind.

Or see if the financial aid office will cc you on these communications. They do this sometimes.

I don't care how you do it, make sure you stay on top of these emails, even if you have to hire a Russian to hack into your kid's emails.

Take it from me, I ignored communications from my lenders for years - monitor all lender emails and letters vigilantly or you could end up racking up interest and fees and other penalties!

CHAPTER 28

AVOID DEADLY STUDENT LOAN TRAPS

This chapter makes my stomach turn. It's by far the most painful part of this book for me to write, because of my own depressing, horrible experience with student loans. Between college and law school, I capped out at close to $100,000.

Actually, it was more, but I paid of my undergrad loans before I went to law school, by bartending two-three jobs, working seven days per week.It was really fun, and lucrative, I'm not complaining. Truthfully, it was a little too much fun, but the party had to end sometime.

I never focused on my loans. It didn't dawn on me or my parents to ask for more free money and less aid. In retrospect, I wish my parents had given me a message other than, "Don't worry, it will all work out."

They sure were wrong – it definitely did NOT work out – I couldn't make the payments. I had all sorts of stress and credit issues, some which still crop up unexpectedly.

Today I hear about kids graduating with $300,000, $500,000, even $800,000 in the case of a newly minted oral surgeon. I don't care how much income you may earn out of medical or dental school, these are HUGE holes to dig out of.

My hope in writing this book – and for being in the college consulting business, for that matter – is to help as many people as humanly possible to avoid what I went through.

For several years since 2008, pundits have predicted that student loans would create the next bubble.

And for good reason – student debt passed consumer debt as the largest category of money owed by Americans – going past the 1.3 Trillion mark in 2016. Defaults are on the rise. Young, entrepreneurial-minded college graduates cite loan payments as the main factor preventing them from starting up a company.

If innovation slows, the long-term effects of the student loan problem could be a lot worse than a bubble.

It's not easy to make payments of $750 per month when you have low or no income and no prospects around the corner. But the best defense is a good offense - be proactive and avoid taking this debt on in the first place, BEFORE you commit to a certain college.

Please be careful about your assumptions that it's "worth" paying up for a brand name college because of its reputation. There is no objective, scientific evidence that Ivy League or equivalent colleges produce more financially successful graduates than their less-competitive sister schools

OK, off the soapbox. Here's a rundown of the most common types of college loans, and their current rates (rates reset every July):

Interest Rates for Direct Loans First Disbursed on or After July 1, 2019, and Before July 1, 2020		
Loan Type	Borrower Type	Fixed Interest Rate
Direct Subsidized Loans and Direct Unsubsidized Loans	Undergraduate	4.53%
Direct Unsubsidized Loans	Graduate or Professional	6.08%
Direct PLUS Loans	Parents and Graduate or Professional Students	7.08%

I pulled this, without anyone's permission[99] at https://studentaid.ed.gov/sa/types/loans/interest-rates#rates

Let's go through these loans, quick like a bunny:

- The Stafford (or "Direct") subsidized loan
- The Stafford (or "Direct") unsubsidized loan[100]
- The PLUS Loan (Parent Loan for Undergraduate Students)
- Private student loans

Direct Loan – Subsidized

---

[99] 'Cause I'm a BADASS!

[100] I'm going to call each of them "Direct" but I'm still mentally calling them "Stafford" loans. I'm so Old School.

These are the most benign of all the loan options available for a few reasons:

- The interest rates are relatively low
- The government pays ("subsidizes") the interest rate until six months after graduation
- Fees are non-existent (practically)
- The amounts you can borrow don't go very far (up to $5,500, usually $3,500 is the maximum)

Students used to apply to third parties for Stafford loans, like banks and other lenders. Now, by going directly to the colleges, students pay lower fees.

Unsubsidized Direct Loan.

The key differences between the Subsidized and Unsubsidized Direct (Stafford) Loans is that the interest on the Unsubsidized Stafford accrues immediately (the government doesn't "subsidize" it)

Combined annual loan limits for each type of Stafford start at $5,500 for freshmen, then increase to $6,500 for sophomores, then $7,500 per year for each remaining year of college.

Perkins Loan

This is primarily for low income families. The interest rate is low (5%), so are the loan amounts –typically $1,000 or so. I don't see a lot of these in my practice.

Here's a great, clear site that explains all this loan stuff, plus a lot of the boring nitty-gritty details I don't want to get bogged down with:

RESOURCE: Everything you wanted to know and did not know that you didn't know, but were afraid to ask about student loans: http://www.finaid.org/loans/studentloan.phtml

(See this site for more details – like how to apply, how to fill out the Master Promissory Note and other information.

Also check out www.StudentLoans.gov - the official site of the Department of Education – for the rest of the story.)

Now let's look at the PLUS loan, one of the worst names in the history of financial products. It's a big fat MINUS for parents.

CHAPTER 29

THE PLUS LOAN

A Subprime Loan from Uncle Sam

Here are the facts on the Parent Loan For Undergraduate Students (PLUS) Loan:

- It is offered by the financial aid office to parents – but it is NOT financial aid – it's a loan product to fill the "gap" between the college's financial aid award to you and the amount you have to cough up.
- It currently carries an interest rate of 7.08% as of 2019, adjusts each July and is capped at 10.5%.
- It's payable over 10 years – making the payments higher than a 30 year mortgage, for example.
- Here's the worst part about the PLUS loan – The Department of Education charges a 4% origination fee on this loan – so if you need to net $100,000, you'll borrow $104,000!

I read that the government makes $55 Billion in profits from lending to students and parents last year, which is more than the earnings of Exxonmobil – the most profitable company in the world, and several of the country's biggest companies combined!)

To be eligible for a PLUS loan:

- You must be the biological or adoptive parent of the student;
- The student must be a dependent (under age 24) enrolled at least half-time;
- You must pass a credit check (less rigorous than applying for a mortgage, though); and
- You must apply with a Master Promissory Note (MPN in financial aid lingo).

The limit is the college's Cost of Attendance less any financial aid it has awarded (that's the "gap" I mentioned before)

Of course this is only a summary. Here's the Department of Education's link for the PLUS and all loans:

https://studentaid.ed.gov/sa/types/loans

CHAPTER 30

PRIVATE STUDENT LOANS

Not quite as sucky as you'd think (but still pretty ugly)

Thanks to our financial meltdown in 2008, there are a LOT fewer choices of private student lenders than before (banks and other lenders that finance college, not the government).

The Consumer Financial Protection Bureau estimated that there are $165 billion in private loans (compared to 1.3 trillion in federal student loans).

Until the law changed in 2013, I thought of private student loans as a last resort. And they still are, for many people, because they are generally high rate (frequently double-digit), high fee, variable – not fixed – instruments.

But I've noticed that some lenders don't charge anywhere near the 4% origination fee that the Department of Education dings you for on the PLUS loan. Many don't charge at all.

And, now that the PLUS loan is variable, some private loans don't look as bad as they used to - if only by comparison. The old hierarchy of financial aid used to be:

1. Grants and Scholarships

2. Work Study/outside employment
3. Stafford Subsidized Loans/Perkins Loans
4. Stafford Unsubsidized Loans
5. Home Equity/Mortgage Loans
6. PLUS Loan
7. Robbing a bank
8. Private Student Loans

Now, I'd flip-flop Private Student Loans and the PLUS loan on a case-by-case basis.

Here are some key concepts you should know about private student loans.

APR

Interest rates are important. But APR – Annualized Percentage Rate – is more important. APR is a formulaic representation of the true cost of your credit – interest rates AND fees – that was designed to allow you to make an apples to apples comparison between loan offers (whether mortgage loans, auto loans or student loans).

Because a lender can '"tease" you with a lower rate but bury fees in the mountains of disclosures you sign, the APR is designed to make this process more "transparent" as the attorneys and regulators say.

You won't know your actual interest rate (and APR) until your loan application has cleared underwriting – meaning they've

159

looked at your credit score, income, other debts, whether you floss regularly and if you're good to your mother. So don't assume an advertised rate is the rate you'll be approved for - it's designed to get you to apply.

How Rates Adjust

These interest rates are almost always variable rates, meaning they adjust at certain junctures. Here is how many of them are calculated (this is complicated but important to understand):

INDEX + MARGIN = RATE

"Index" refers to a benchmark, or measurement like LIBOR – a rate set by European banks that is similar to the Prime Rate. This is also the cost of money to the student lender.

"Margin" means the profit. It's added to the Index by lenders.

Let's say that this index – LIBOR – is currently .5% and the margin is 7, your rate is 7.5%.(Index + Margin).

The better your credit history, the lower the perceived risk to the lender – and the lower your margin. Your interest rate and APR should be lower. You'll pay less.

If you have some dings on your credit, your margin, and interest rate will be higher, because you represent a higher risk.

Co-signing

If you must co-sign for your child (almost always required), check if the terms allow you to be dropped as a guarantor after a certain history of on-time payments – typically two years.

Look at the flexibility of payment terms – some loans allow you to defer payments until after you graduate, some require payments even though your child is in college.

Ask for discounts – sometimes student lenders will lower the interest rate if you sign up for auto-debits that come right out of your checking account – probably around ¼ of 1%. I'm not a big fan of this but you may be more comfortable with giving access to your bank account!

Be wary of college "Preferred Lender Lists." Although not as common as in the past, many colleges would publish a list of four-10 lenders on their site as "Preferred Lenders."

I hope you're sitting down before I lay this one on you....these colleges would get referral fees[101] for sending applicants to the lenders on the Preferred Lender list! So just because a college prefers a lender does not mean that you should.

Here is an objective listing, alphabetically, of student lenders right from the Finaid.org website:

http://www.finaid.org/loans/privatestudentloans.phtml

---

[101] "Kick back" is such a vulgar term.

Another site that we visit frequently on behalf of our clients is www.SimpleTuition.com, , owned by Bank Rate. You plug in your income and other financial information, then sit back and let the loan solicitations fly into your inbox. Fun!

RESOURCE: The best defense against paying excessive interest and fees to a student lender is a good offense - learn how to triple your eligibility for aid, even if you think you're situation is hopeless: www.FinancialAidWebcast.com

CHAPTER 31

HOW MUCH MONEY DO GRADS OF ELITE COLLEGES MAKE?

Is it worth "paying up?" for an Ivy?

According to widespread opinion, brainwashing by the colleges themselves and lore, graduates of the most selective colleges earn more than those who graduated from the least selective schools. There's more to this argument than meets the eye.

Think about it: wouldn't you assume that the hardest working, most motivated kids would tend to apply to the toughest schools to get into? Perhaps they would be successful no matter where they went to college.

In fact, that's what two studies by economists Stacy Dale and Alan Kreuger seem to indicate. There's little to no evidence that similarly credentialed kids (SAT scores and GPA) earn more money if they attend an Ivy or other highly selective college compared to similar kids who graduated from "regular" colleges.

I've written about this in another book, *How to Get Into Your Dream College Without Lying, Bribing or Photoshopping,*[102] but

---

[102] Makes a WONDERFUL holiday gift. Just sayin.' Again. Available on Amazon!

I'm happy to nutshell the main point here just in case you're too much of a tightwad to buy yourself and 12 of your closest friends copies.

Check out this list of colleges, ranked by salary potential on Payscale.com (I won't lie, I never heard of #15):

1. Harvey Mudd
2. Princeton
3. MIT
4. SUNY Maritime
5. US Military Academy
6. US Naval Academy
7. Cal Tech
8. Babson College
9. Harvard
10. Stanford
11. Dartmouth
12. Williams
13. Air Force Academy
14. Webb Institute
15. Samuel Merritt University

Source: https://www.payscale.com/college-salary-report/bachelors

CHAPTER 32

GENEROUS SCHOOLS FOR B STUDENTS

I've gotten questions like "It seems like your advice is only for super high achieving kids. I have a "normal" child – will your stuff work for him?"

Most of my clients are in the A minus neighborhood. Maybe 10% or so are super high achievers, and 5% fall into the B to B minus or lower category.

Here's a great list – it comes from the website, DIYCollegeRankings.com (highly recommended). These schools each admit more than 50% of applicants and give grants to 97-100% of freshman, averaging $17,000 plus per:

Assumption College

Hood College

Albion College

College of Saint Benedict

Saint John's University

Gustavus Adolphus College

Hamline University

William Jewell College

Millsaps College

Salem College

Creighton University

Colby-Sawyer College

Saint Anselm College

Elmira College

Clarkson University

Niagara University

Saint Bonaventure University

Wagner College

Canisius College

Xavier University

Ohio Wesleyan University

The College of Wooster

John Carroll University

Capital University

Wittenberg University

Pacific University

Saint Vincent College

Chatham University

Westminster College

Allegheny College

Lycoming College

Arcadia University

Juniata College

Ursinus College

The University of the Arts

La Salle University

Elizabethtown College

Susquehanna University

Erskine College and Seminary

Presbyterian College

Maryville College

University of Dallas

Austin College

Randolph College

Randolph-Macon College

Sweet Briar College

Hollins University

Bridgewater College

Hampden-Sydney College

Roanoke College

Saint Michael's College

Lawrence University

Beloit College

Wheeling Jesuit University

CHAPTER 33

THE 20 MOST EXPENSIVE COLLEGES

Look at college tuition numbers, and you might have a few reactions:

Jesus, I can't believe how much they charge!

Or, *Those numbers don't seem that bad...WAIT - they're TUITION-ONLY numbers – not including room and board? Sweet mother of Jesus!*

Or, *Why are they all within a few dollars of each other?*

If it's any consolation, I've had each of these thoughts. Check out this list from the College Affordability And Transparency Center: The most expensive colleges, by tuition (this list may have changed a smidge since the last edition of this book, but I'm honestly too lazy to update it):

Highest Tuition Colleges

Columbia University in the City of New York	$53,000
University of Chicago	$51,351
Landmark College	$51,330
Vassar College	$51,250
Sarah Lawrence College	$51,038
Trinity College	$50,776
Carnegie Mellon University	$50,665
Harvey Mudd College	$50,649
Tufts University	$50,604
Oberlin College	$50,582
Amherst College	$50,562
George Washington University	$50,435
Franklin and Marshall College	$50,400
University of Southern California	$50,277
Bard College at Simon's Rock	$50,209
Bucknell University	$50,152
Williams College	$50,070
Union College	$50,013
Colgate University	$49,970
Reed College	$49,940
Bard College	$49,906
Hobart William Smith Colleges	$49,677
St. John's College	$49,644
Tulane University of Louisiana	$49,638
Brandeis University	$49,598

University of Pennsylvania	$49,536
Dartmouth College	$49,506
Hamilton College	$49,500
Dickinson College	$49,489
St Lawrence University	$49,420
Connecticut College	$49,350
Brown University	$49,346
Rensselaer Polytechnic Institute	$49,341
Boston College	$49,324
Wesleyan University	$49,274
Carleton College	$49,263
Occidental College	$49,248
Duke University	$49,241
Scripps College	$49,152
Gettysburg College	$49,140
Kenyon College	$49,140
Colby College	$49,120
Skidmore College	$49,120
St John's College	$49,119
Cornell University	$49,116
Haverford College	$49,098
Hampshire College	$49,048
Northwestern University	$49,047
Claremont McKenna College	$49,045
Colorado College	$48,996
Macalester College	$48,887
Drexel University	$48,791

Johns Hopkins University	$48,710
Pitzer College	$48,670
Georgetown University	$48,611
Boston University	$48,436
Bates College	$48,435
Pepperdine University	$48,342
University of Rochester	$48,280
Bennington College	$48,220
Bowdoin College	$48,212
Southern Methodist University	$48,190
Franklin W Olin College of Engineering	$48,181
Washington University in St Louis	$48,093
University of Richmond	$48,090
University of Notre Dame	$47,929
Middlebury College	$47,823

Most of the colleges on this list offer hefty tuition discounts however, so you shouldn't be misled by tuition only.

So now, let's look at the highest NET PRICES charged (also not updated since the 2018-2019 book L-A-Z-Y.).

Spoiler alert: lots 'o art schools! And some snooty private colleges that you'll be quite familiar with!

Highest Net Price Colleges

Southern California Institute of Architecture	$48,730

California Institute of the Arts	$47,362
The Boston Conservatory	$45,272
San Francisco Art Institute	$44,999
School of the Art Institute of Chicago	$44,378
Art Center College of Design	$43,775
The New School	$43,328
Ringling College of Art and Design	$42,532
Jewish Theological Seminary of America	$42,416
Berklee College of Music	$42,338
School of the Museum of Fine Arts-Boston	$41,554
Cooper Union for the Advancement of Science and Art	$40,617
Drexel University	$40,615
The New England Conservatory of Music	$40,557
Oberlin College	$40,550
Loyola Marymount University	$40,226
Rose-Hulman Institute of Technology	$40,198
Pratt Institute-Main	$40,133
Maryland Institute College of Art	$39,718
University of Puget Sound	$39,662
Worcester Polytechnic Institute	$39,011
Savannah College of Art and Design	$38,645
Sacred Heart University	$38,313
Pennsylvania Academy of the Fine Arts	$38,267
Hobart William Smith Colleges	$38,243
Otis College of Art and Design	$38,141
Beacon College	$38,054

Rhode Island School of Design	$37,949
Rensselaer Polytechnic Institute	$37,820
Bard College at Simon's Rock	$37,618
California College of the Arts	$37,587
Sarah Lawrence College	$37,422
George Washington University	$37,404
Union College	$37,358
Cleveland Institute of Music	$37,259
Santa Clara University	$37,198
Saint Joseph's University	$37,191
American Musical and Dramatic Academy	$37,069
Landmark College	$36,984
High Point University	$36,927
Whitman College	$36,894
Lynn University	$36,880
Emerson College	$36,720
Chapman University	$36,602
Southern Methodist University	$36,602
Fairfield University	$36,598
Catholic University of America	$36,585
Cleveland University-Kansas City	$36,435
Longy School of Music of Bard College	$36,405
Bryant University	$36,109
MCPHS University	$36,043
New York School of Interior Design	$36,034
University of San Diego	$35,950
Fordham University	$35,912

Roger Williams University	$35,755
Bucknell University	$35,677
University of San Francisco	$35,641
Quinnipiac University	$35,595
Marist College	$35,586
University of Miami	$35,444
Seattle University	$35,261
Scripps College	$35,211
Cornish College of the Arts	$35,146
Marymount Manhattan College	$35,117
New York University	$35,106

Please consult this and other info on the College Affordability site before you finalize your college list:

RESOURCE: The College Affordability And Transparency Center (Department Of Education)
http://collegecost.ed.gov/catc/#

CHAPTER 34

ADDENDUM: FREE COLLEGE FOR NEW YORKERS

In 2017, Governor Andy Boy Cuomo rolled out, with much fanfare, his "Excelsior" scholarship program, a/k/a Free College!

But it's not exactly "free-free." The program covers tuition at a State University of New York college, which equates to approximately $7,000 of the total cost of attendance, or $26,000 plus.

Further, Excelsior covers *up to* $7,000 for families, inclusive of other aid they may have qualified for from the federal and state governments, including the Pell grant and the New York Tuition Assistance Program (TAP).

In other words, if a qualifying family receives a $5,000 Pell grant, they can also get a maximum of $2,000 under Excelsior (as opposed to an additional $7,000 on top of the $5,000 Pell grant).

Here are the Excelsior guidelines. To qualify, applicants must:

- be a resident of NYS and have resided in NYS for 12 continuous months prior to the beginning of the term;
- be a U.S. citizen or eligible non-citizen;

- have either graduated from high school in the United States, earned a high school equivalency diploma, or passed a federally approved "Ability to Benefit" test, as defined by the Commissioner of the State Education Department;

- have a combined federal adjusted gross income of $100,000 or less (Note from Andy: $110,000 in 2018 and $125,000 thereafter);

- be pursuing an undergraduate degree at a SUNY or CUNY college, including community colleges and the statutory colleges at Cornell University and Alfred University;

- be enrolled in at least 12 credits per term and complete at least 30 credits each year (successively), applicable toward his or her degree program;

- if attended college prior to the 2017-18 academic year, have earned at least 30 credits each year (successively), applicable toward his or her degree program prior to applying for an Excelsior Scholarship;

- be in a non-default status on a student loan made under any NYS or federal education loan program or on the repayment of any NYS award;

- be in compliance with the terms of the service condition(s) imposed by a NYS award that you have previously received; and

- execute a Contract agreeing to reside in NYS for the length of time the award was received, and, if employed during such time, be employed in NYS. (Note from Andy: If you go to college for four years under the Excelsior program, you must work in New York for four consecutive years after graduation. If you do not, your free benefit turns into a loan for the period of time you "owe" New York.)

180

It's too early to see what, if any fallout there could be or how well this initiative will actually work. I wonder if it will become harder for New Yorkers to get into SUNY and CUNY colleges. I also do not know the terms of the loan that the free tuition benefits converts to should the college grad leave New York to work before their obligation period ends.

We'll have to see what happens!

CONCLUSION

Now what? What you should do next.

Now you possess an impressive arsenal of money-saving tips and strategies about how to play the financial aid game to win. You have also learned about several of money-sucking "landmines" to avoid.

This book is general advice, and necessarily incomplete. I did not hold back any key information, and attempted to make this book easy to read and use, as opposed to a dry, scholarly textbook that stinks to read...and write.

But let's talk turkey: this information is merely a starting point. The saying is "Knowledge is power," but that's misleading.

Knowledge is useless without IMPLEMENTATION. You must use your newly-discovered super powers if you want to benefit from them. So here is a summary of what we covered, and some homework.

1. Research the historical generosity of every school on your list. Use the Common Data Set, the College Board and the Net Price Calculators.

2. Determine how colleges meet financial need – the percentage that's free and the amount that's loans/work study. Same resources.

3. Calculate your EFC and how you can lower just by shifting your savings from non-exempt assets into exempt assets. See www.FinancialAidWebcast.com and www.Facebook.com/lockwoodcollegeprep for more free information, including our live shows, our podcasts and webinars.

4. If you're going to "shelter" your assets, make sure you understand the actual and potential negative consequences: taxes, potential penalties, not to mention the features of any exempt financial instrument you use to implement one of the strategies in this book or anything you stumble across.

5. Know your priority deadlines. Check out the website for EACH college on your list.

6. Even if you make seven figures, there's a lot of money available for you - if you apply to schools STRATEGICALLY, not only Rear Window Sticker Colleges.

7. Don't give up if you've received a lousy award – you might be able to improve it: AppealsClass.com

I hope you feel better about tackling this overly-complicated, intimidating, high-stakes process!

Special offer from Moi to You

If, after you've diligently combed your way through this book, you still have questions about your own personal college financial plan, I'm happy to chat with you, no charge, for 20 minutes on the phone for a "College Strategy Session. (I bill at $1,000 per hour so you have made an incredible amount of money by booking a call with me, gratis! :)

Go to www.BookLockwood.com to book your phone call to discuss strategy and whether you could be a good fit for one of our programs. College advising programs start at $5,000, help with only the financial aid portion is less.

Or, you can shoot me an email at "wholesale@lockwoodcollegeprep.com. That's a real email address, that I actually reply to.

Let me know how you're doing and what you think of this book!

Good luck in all things college!

Andy Lockwood, J.D.
Lockwood College Prep
135 Glenwood Road
Glenwood Landing, New York 11547-0535
516-882-5464
www.LockwoodCollegePrep.com

ABOUT ANDY LOCKWOOD

Andy Lockwood is a controversial, outspoken critic of runaway college costs and a college admissions and finance consultant. He specializes in helping select high school students get into their Dream Colleges, and "Forgotten Middle Class" families take advantage of legal and ethical loopholes in the federal financial aid system so that they can pay for a top college without filing bankruptcy or being forced to eat mac 'n cheese every night.

Daily, Andy witnesses first-hand the stress and emotional roller coaster felt by parents of college-bound children caused by outrageous, skyrocketing bills from America's top colleges.

A highly sought after and entertaining (to himself) public speaker, Andy lectures several times a month on college planning "secrets" at libraries and high schools, PTA/PTO's, financial planners, numerous Temples, Jewish Community Centers and other civic and religious organizations. Andy currently hosts and publishes the *College Planning Edge* podcast, available on iTunes, and *College Talk Tuesday* and *College Coffee Talk*, on his Facebook page, www.Facedbook.com/LockwoodCollegePrep .

Andy chose his career because he personally amassed more than $100,000 in student debt between undergraduate studies at Wesleyan University, where he was a member[103] of the basketball

---

[103] "Played" would be artistic license.

team – and St. John's University School of Law. Now, he and his wife, Pearl, have sworn a blood oath that they will never allow their four children to go through what he endured.

Before becoming an entrepreneur, Andy practiced corporate law, where he was responsible for closing transactions of $500,000,000 and up, served as in-house counsel to a publicly traded broker-dealer and as a member of the board of directors of a publicly-traded education company.

Andy is a member of the New York State Financial Aid Administrators' Association (NYSFAA) and writes a college planning column for *North Shore Today*, a local publication in Long Island, New York.

A native of Newton, Massachusetts, Andy is a die-hard fan of the Red Sox, Celtics, Patriots and other teams hated by New Yorkers.

If you are interested in having Andy speak to your parent group or interested in his company's financial aid forms preparation, college coaching, ACT/SAT tutoring or other services, please contact his office at 516-882-5464, or email "wholesale@lockwoodcollegeprep.com or visit www.LockwoodCollegePrep.com.

TESTIMONIALS

From the minute I walked in your door for the first time, I felt an enormous weight had been lifted off me. Thank you for all that you have done to help me and my precious girls.

- Beth Freeman

Scottsdale, Arizona

# # #

Just to let you know that I am spreading the word about Andy coming to GCHS in May and that many of our parents and students should attend. I was a fan but now I know how much work you guys do and how helpful it is. Well worth the money.

Mary Ellen Cuomo

Teacher, Key Club Advisor, Glen Cove High School

North Shore High School SEPTA Board Member

# # #

What more could you possibly ask for? Incredibly insightful and helpful advice delivered concisely and humorously. Andy Lockwood has the credentials, the experience, the wisdom, the strong work ethic and a true sense of honesty. As far as I'm concerned, if you want to pay less for college....read Andy's book....then call the guy. He's the same in person only taller.

Randy Levin – College Essay Specialist

Hi Andy,

Thank you for your guidebook. Normally I have to suffer through a variety of dry college guides and references in order to get updated information on the college and financial aid process. Your style of writing made it not only easy to read, but it made me laugh along the way. Not being an expert in the financial aid process, I felt your explanation provided a no-nonsense breakdown on the best methods in planning to pay for college. During my college planning meetings, I feel comfortable recommending your book to my parents to assist in their financial planning.

Sincerely

Mike

Guidance Counselor

Long Island

Dear Andy,

I wanted to send you a letter thanking you for all of your help over the past few months. From the time I went to your seminar I felt so much more comfortable in what I had to do and how the whole process of applying for financial aid /scholarships worked.

It literally was a huge relief knowing that there was help out there and you guided us step by step. You saved me thousands of dollars that will enable me to lose a little less sleep.

Thanks for your help, guidance and for always being there when I had dozens of questions. The bad part for you is that with my two other children you will have to deal with me for the next 10 years, good luck with that.

Sincerely yours

Michael Levy

Roslyn, New York

#

I told them I don't want to play games with my money or get some extra bill in the future. They promised I would get back five times what I invested for the service.

They were true to their word.

 Debbie & Terry Cooney

Davie, Florida

#

Dear Andy:

We wanted to let you know Clark selected Georgia Tech and is starting engineering school there in August.

Thank you so much for your support and guidance and expert advice during this collegiate process.

Peter Strugatz

Carrie Clark

Easthampton, New York

#

I came away from our meeting thinking, "How can I NOT afford to hire Andy!"

Ralph Rizzuto

Huntington, New York

#

Dear Andy,

I just wanted to thank you again for your help.

We knew that our financial situation was a little complicated to explain and so originally went to another college finance consultant for assistance. Despite his help, our application for aid was rejected and our joy at our son's acceptance to his school of first choice turned into panic. I didn't know how we could pay the full amount, over $60,000 per year, without jeopardizing our other children's educational options. It was about that time that I attended one of your free lectures and realized we might still have a chance. I was impressed with your clear, no nonsense approach and decided to try again.

You took considerable time going over all our financials and business history and then gave us excellent advice. Your quick grasp of the issues, optimism, easy manner and expertise were reassuring and invaluable. Thanks to your efforts, we were able to receive the financial aid we needed, almost $15,000, even though we had already been turned down once before.

We're very grateful for your help and wouldn't hesitate for a minute to recommend you to our friends. I'm only sorry we didn't go to you first.

Sincere regards,

[Name withheld for publication out of paranoia that client's son's Ivy League college will discover this somehow and reduce his award]

# # #

My son was admitted to Tulane University and received an extremely generous aid package. I strongly believe that what I learned from you was a big part of it.

Mitchell Fein

Great Neck, New York

# # #

I met with you - you told me that you couldn't help me and not to waste my money. That's when I knew you were an honest guy!

Anthony DiBattista

New Hyde Park, NY

# # #

I don't know where to begin. Our financial aid packages are just now starting to come in and each one is better than the next. Just today Boston University gave is $40,000. Rob and I had no idea how were were possibly going to afford to send our girls to college. Thanks to your knowledge of filing and the FAFSA and CSS form, and your strategic positioning of our finances, we're now comfortable in knowing we are getting the most out of the system and will be able to put our girls through college. Thank you Andy! You made this process so easy and, dare I say, downright fun...you helped us afford our kids' dream schools. Thank goodness you know all the loopholes.

Very truly yours,

Stephanie and Rob Salzbank

Port Washington, NY

# # #

My son is going to a top college (George Washington) on monies he received totally from Andy's involvement. He looked me in the eye and told me...'I get my clients five times the amount of their investment. HE WASN'T KIDDING!!! Best money I ever spent.

Scott Sanders

Long Beach, NY

Dear Andy

I finally have a moment to thank you for all your help this year. I know that my circumstances are unusual. You pushed me outside of my comfort zone in order to financially benefit. And it worked! If you weren't beside me cheering me on, I would not have had the courage to approach the financial aid department at Syracuse - twice! You have been great throughout this experience.

Thanks again,

Diane

Bellmore

Dear Andy,

I wanted to thank you for all the help you have given me regarding my son Robert's financial planning for college.

You were an enormous help when I had problems with the FAFSA and eventually the appeal to SUNY Albany.

Your professionalism and patience is what makes you and your business so successful.

I am going to recommend you to all my friends so they can put their mind at ease and not have to worry about undertaking this daunting process alone!

Sincerely,

Sabrina Ferrara

Hauppauge, NY

# # #

Andy Lockwood and Staff

Dear Mr. Lockwood,

I would like to thank Andy and his staff, and provide affirmation that Andy's program works and is proven to be successful. Entering into our journey regarding how we will possibly be able to fund an annual expense of $30K plus is an overwhelming mental experience. The typical family needs guidance and direction from a qualified individual and Andy is the person to do just that. Andy provided mental relief and was able to provide a strategy when completing the necessary details for the FAFSA. Andy provided clear cut direction based on his knowledge and awareness of financial aid available to most families regardless of financial status. Andy personally engagement in the process regarding the submission of the documents to the educational institutions of choice and provided an estimate of financial aid so there that there was an expectation, which allows for a family to plan accordingly. Due to Andy's experience and knowledge regarding available financial aid, the process of developing a plan to support my son's financial needs for his college education was actual a pleasant experience and not one of hardship and despair.

Once again thanks, Andy to you and your staff and the continued support in making this process a rewarding experience.

We have recommended your firm to a number of our family friends and we are grateful that we were able to have the opportunity to work closely with you on this very important milestone in my son's next step in life.

Most Sincerely

Sean Cunningham

Belleville, NJ

# # #

Please express my gratitude to Andy. My son qualified for very generous financial aid packages so far from the colleges we heard from. We are very happy and pleased!

If he mails me his business cards when he mails me back my tax information We will give them out to a few people whom we know really will benefit from his services, or possibly sponsor a seminar if he is interested.

Thanks again

Darlene

Locust Valley, NY

#

Andy,

We want to thank you and Pearl for all your hard work handling our daughter's financial aid forms and advising us on the issues surrounding college admission. You simplified an often complex process and took a huge load off of our shoulders. While we should have listened to your advice regarding early decision, we were pleased with the increase in financial aid afforded to us. We look forward to your counsel in the years ahead for all three of our college bound children. It's great working with you both.

Jeanne & Gary Lofgren

Westbury, NY

#

The Weston High School PTO hosted Andy for an extremely informative and entertaining seminar on the best-kept secrets of securing the ideal financial aid package.

Weston is home to a high income parent population and most walked away not just pleased but astonished that they could, in fact, qualify for financial aid!

The PTO received terrific feedback and we are looking forward to having Andy back next year -- kudos to Andy for a job well done!

Lisa Bigelow

Vice President, Weston (Connecticut) High School PTO

# # #

I saw Andy's ad I was impressed with his knowledge of the whole financial aid process and very happy with the service he provides.

Initially, I thought I was just going to get financial aid advice but Andy helped us with a lot more than that. He spoke about camps Alexis should attend to showcase her talents, the sports resume to send out to colleges, sports DVD, the essays she should be writing, internships and just so many other little details that I just didn't think about. His rolodex is filled with the right connections that Lexi needed for the college process. He helped us market our daughter.

I think it would be worth your time to meet with Andy.

Thank you,

Karen Greene

Glen Head, New York

I met with my Teen Advisory Group on Tuesday and they told me they really enjoyed your presentation especially that you geared it for "the forgotten middle class", and gave them tips and information that they could easily understand. They also liked your sense of humor and jokes and thought they enhanced an already fine presentation.

Just wanted to let you know that I have you scheduled for a "College Finance Secrets" program...We are looking forward to your program, and I will be in touch a few weeks beforehand.

Sincerely,

Cathy Loechner,

Young Adult Librarian

Shelter Rock Public Library

516-248-7363 ext. 239

###

Lisa, Please thank Andy Lockwood for his wonderful presentation at our recent Board Meeting. We found it very informative and helpful.

I am sure a lot of the parents who attended the presentation will be following up with him for subsequent meetings.

Thanks again,

Lisa Edelblum

President, Roslyn High School Parent Faculty Association

# # #

Mr. Lockwood has presented several informative workshops at The Bryant Library in Roslyn over the past few years. Despite the dry subject matter of the college financial aid process, Mr. Lockwood engages the audience with both humor and honesty. His knowledge on an often confusing subject is evident during his workshop and parents are often eager to learn more from Mr. Lockwood.

Lauren Fazio -

Young Adult Librarian

The Bryant Library (Roslyn NY)

# # #

My library page told me her dad attended and said you were very good, better than the guy that had come here last year, {local businessman). I also just got off the phone with a parent that called and thanked me for running your program. She said she and the other parents got a lot of good information and that you were a wonderful speaker and very animated. I told her I would make an effort to have you come back in the spring!

High marks indeed!

Thank you again!

Linda Meglio

Young Adult Librarian

Greenlawn Public Library

#

...My daughter's long and incongruent "wish list" quickly evolved into ten schools -three in-state and seven out of state , two back ups," the core choices and one stretch school. She was confident and focused as she plunged into the applications. With your guidance, she wrote some terrific essays and completed all ten on time. While all of this was going on you magically expedited the FAFSA and other financial paperwork to all the schools taking that burden and administrative nightmare off our shoulders.

The proof of your program was she was accepted at seven Top 100 schools four of which were out of state, waitlisted at two out of states and was only declined at the "stretch" school, Georgetown. As it turned out, the first school to reply was the one she finally chose but that was only decided once we had all the offers in hand. Every single school made very generous scholarship offers and we ended up choosing a Top 30 school that offered 95% of the total cost of attendance, 70% of which was free money!

We look forward to the next 4 years and our next child knowing that we have the College Planners on our team. Thanks again, Andy and Pete - it has been a pleasure working with you.

Regards,

Tom Browne

Weston, Florida

#

"The only thing trickier than applying to college is paying for it. That's why "Never Pay Retail for College" is so valuable. It takes readers through strategies they won't find elsewhere to reduce the burden of paying the pipers at America's colleges and universities. This book will pay for itself, many times over, and should be on the hard drive of any parents with college-bound kids."

– Matt Rees, Editor, FT Newsmine – a Financial Times publication, former Speechwriter for the Executive Office of the President, The Securities and Exchange Commission and the

Secretary of the Treasury, Writer for The Wall Street Journal, The New York Times, The Economist and The Washington Post.

# # #

Families are faced with two very challenging hurdles as the first decade of the 21st Century nears a close: Where they can gain perspective and education on how to retire in the style they desire, and how to give their children the best chance to survive their own generation's financial challenges. It starts with a solid education. This book, by clearly defining the challenges and presenting some of the opportunities for those families, starts them on the road to addressing the latter challenge. By doing so, it may just help them move closer to achieving the former as well.

– Robert Isbitts, Author of "Wall Street Bull and How to Bear It", Chief Investment Officer, Emerald Asset Advisors and Worth Magazine's Top 100 Wealth Advisors

# # #

Like all parts of personal finance paying for college is becoming increasingly complex. Colleges are businesses that go through ups and downs like any other business. With endowments from private schools posting record breaking declines and 48 out of 50 states currently confronting budget deficits the costs for both private and public colleges are likely to keep going up at a rate faster than inflation.

Every parent regardless of income level should be going after financial aid and Never Pay Retail For College is exactly the tool to help people learn the strategic ins and outs of every aspect of planning, applying and negotiating for college aid. There are 70 factors that go into determining aid packages, can you even name four? Never Pay Retail For College also debunks numerous myths about college like private school potentially being cheaper than public schools. Maybe you don't know how that can be but the authors of Never Pay Retail For College do.

– Roger Nussbaum, Chief Investment Officer, Your Source Financial, Phoenix, Arizona, (commentator on CNBC – Asia, publisher of RandomRoger.com)

# # #

Dear Mr. Lockwood

I am writing this letter to recommend your services to any parent that has a son or daughter approaching college. We received guidance for career choices, college selection and obtained financial aid advice from College Planning Specialists.

The financial aid award we received was much greater than we had envisioned.

Mr. Lockwood is knowledgeable, professional and very accommodating to work with.

Please consult with him

Very truly yours,

Douglas P. Johnson

Attorney–at–law

Davie, Florida

# # #

Hello Andy,

How are you doing? I have some good news!!! U Miami's Office of Financial aid finally revised Farley's fafsa and financial aid package and gave us more money. I went from receiving 4,600 to receiving 13,730 and they also sent 4,000 back to my sallie mae loan. I'm so happy!! Thank you soo much!!!

Filberta LeTang

Miami, Florida

# # #

Dear College Pete and Andy:

We wanted to express our thanks and gratitude for your professional guidance in the college financial planning process. We first met with you at one of your seminars when Lauren was in the beginning of 10th grade. While initially it seemed perhaps to be a bit premature to plan for college three years in advance, it became clear that in fact that was the perfect time to start planning. You never made any guarantees other than that if we followed your strategies we would put ourselves in the best possible position to be eligible for financial assistance.

We had saved some money for college and had participated in the Florida Prepaid Plan, however we knew that if Lauren chose to go to a private university those funds would be grossly inadequate. Over the course of the next two and one half years we met with you from time to time to map out and plan the best strategy, so when the time came to apply for financial aid, we would be ready.

It became clear that Lauren wanted to go to a private school and in fact her top choice was Vanderbilt University. A prestigious school with a lofty sticker price ($58,000+). The good news was that Vanderbilt stated that they will meet 100% of demonstrated need. With that in mind, and with your financial strategies in hand, we felt confident that Lauren would be eligible for a significant financial aid award. We felt so confident of this that we allowed Lauren to apply to Vanderbilt early decision. It should be noted that Pete mentioned more than once, that applying early decision might be statistically favorable in terms of admission, but could reduce our ability to negotiate financial aid if our initial award was low. (Smells like a disclaimer from College Pete).

Lauren received a letter from Vanderbilt approximately one month ago. The good news for her was that she was accepted for admission. This wonderful news was tempered by the fact that Vanderbilt's initial award for financial aid was approximately

$9,000. Although $9,000 is nice, it clearly was significantly less than what we were expecting. Over the next week, I followed Pete's advice on how to approach Vanderbilt's financial aid office and immediately contacted them to receive clarification on what the basis of the "low" award was. It became clear that Vanderbilt misconstrued some information on our tax return, and Pete, my accountant, and I worked closely together to further explain the tax situation. Ultimately, through perseverance and continued support from Pete the initial award was increased from $9,000.00 to $39,000. We are thrilled as parents as is our daughter, Lauren.

We would highly recommend your professional service to any family who is considering sending their child to a private university.

David and Lisa Reiser

# # #

Thank you for your guidance during this process. You and Pearl made it very easy.

 Alan Karul

Plainview, New York

# # #

Thanks again for all your help - whenever I have a chance to speak to friends who have children with college ahead I recommend your services.

Regards,

Frank Brecher

Commack, New York

#

David was accepted at his first-choice school and we did indeed receive a very generous aid award, with no student loans required first year.

Thanks for your advice and for the information we received through your counseling, your book and the various online resources.

John Rivior

Huntington Station

New York

#

Hi Andy:

Two things that I have learned over the years:

1. Hiring a specialist to assist you in navigating stuff you are not an expert in (you are a specialist as am I. I am coming to you for your expertise in the arena of colleges - you do that every day, you are an expert. Companies come to me to place their

catastrophic risks- where I am an expert). I apply this in my business and personal life.

2. Referral Business is my lifeline. If I do a good job for one guy he tells someone else. My best new business sources are from referrals and people who have done business with me in the past. So yes, if you do a good job for me I will brag to my friends about it.

I will admit that I was a little skeptical at first but awfully glad that we engaged your services I know that we have a ways to go but the first blush looks really great. [EDITOR'S NOTE: Kelly received an $96,000 scholarship offer from one of her two top choice schools.]

I sincerely appreciate you engaging Kelly, I wanted her to be the one to take the lead and responsibility for her own destiny. Having her accountable to someone else besides her Mom (and Dad) was a motivating factor. She was happy to have completed her essay over the summer and gotten an early leg up on the application process. Some of her friends have not even completed essays yet never mind applying to colleges.

Have a great Thanksgiving you and Pearl and the kids!

Theresa Lally

Syosset, New York

# # #